Other Books by Beryl D. Cohon

GOD'S ANGRY MEN

BUTENSKY, *UNIVERSAL PEACE*

And they shall beat their swords into plowshares . . .
See Isaiah 2.2–4; 11

GOD'S
ANGRY
MEN

*A Student's Introduction
to the Hebrew Prophets*

BERYL D. COHON

BLOCH PUBLISHING COMPANY
NEW YORK

ACKNOWLEDGMENT

I owe thanks to two cherished friends and colleagues in the Temple Sinai Religious School, Miss Esther D. Starr, Principal, and Mr. Arnold A. Rubin, for reading the manuscript closely and giving me the benefit of their judgments. Mr. Rubin tried chapters of the book in his classes "for size"; the reactions of the students, and of several younger children, were lively and helpful.

Jules Leon Butensky's *Universal Peace* is reproduced by courtesy of The Metropolitan Museum of Art, Gift of Jacob H. Schiff, 1910.

BERYL D. COHON

Brookline, Massachusetts
August, 1961

A Word to the Teacher

The present book is intended for the secondary level of the Jewish religious schools. It is basically a recreation of the author's *The Prophets: Their Personalities and Teachings*, which he offers as the teacher's book.[1] The primary source, of course, is the Bible.

The effort made here is to present the Hebrew literary prophets as creative and compelling personalities, in a specific setting in history, as protagonists of basic ideals urgent in their time and imperative in our own day. The author has sought to avoid oversimplification and vague generalization at the one extreme, and academically dry and encyclopedic presentations at the other.

Through the Topics for Further Study and Discussion following each chapter, he hopes to help the teacher adapt the material to the level of maturity of the class and to make the prophets relevant to our time. The teacher will not wish to use all the topics suggested for further study and discussion. These are to be selected and adapted to the capacity of the class and to the teaching schedule for the year. The teacher will, of course, bring to the class his or her own topics for discussion. It is hoped that the teacher will select topics for discussion from the disturbed life of our time.

The author wishes to call the teacher's special attention to the following considerations:

A *Who's Who*, a *Chronology*, and a *Map* are invaluable to

[1] Bloch Pub. Co., New York, 1960

help the student fix in his mind the factual backgrounds needed for an understanding of the prophets. They are old devices ever useful. The suggestion is made that these should be built chapter by chapter, as the student advances in the book and in the year's work. At the end of the year, combining the *Who's Who* and the *Chronology* and placing the prophets in their proper places by means of brackets, will bring the history into focus for the young student. The map need not be too detailed; it should give the student the lay of the land, so that when he reads of Jerusalem, Assyria, Babylon, etc., he will have a reasonable orientation.

Dramatization, especially in view of the television experience of our young people, should be helpful and encourage the more gifted students to original creativity. Art work may be encouraged at a good many points in the dramatic stories of the prophets: Amos at Beth-El, Isaiah in the Temple, Jeremiah observing the potter at the wheel, the bold metaphors in Ezekiel, etc. The text affords a rich variety of subject matter.

The musically gifted children should be encouraged to explore the possibility of setting to music some of the singable passages in Isaiah, Jeremiah, Deutero-Isaiah. It might be helpful to consult a well informed choir master; some of this material has been set to music as anthems. Recordings of some of these may be found without too much difficulty.

Paraphrasing prophetic utterance — as, for example, Jeremiah's Temple Sermon — should help students penetrate to the prophet's meaning, and should lead to an appreciation of his vocabulary. The author has sought to retain some of the rugged words and phrases of the prophetic literature through the quotations and through paraphrase.

Memorization of great texts is invaluable. Our young students have an astonishing, and despairing, capacity for forgetting. Memorization helps retain and assimilate choice phrases and sentences. To some these will be a precious possession for a lifetime.

The teacher's book gives a bibliography for the teacher. The author wishes to call special attention to an additional volume, invaluable for its excellent maps and illustrations: *Lands of the Bible — A Golden Historical Atlas* (Simon and Schuster, N.Y.). The historic summaries are excellent. The volume provides, also, a convenient chronology.

TABLE OF CONTENTS

1. PROPHETS AND FORTUNE TELLERS

WE BEGIN our study of the Hebrew prophets with three stories, each from the Bible. The first is about the "false prophets," whom we call "fortune tellers"; the second reports how the true prophet thought and acted; the third tells of the conduct of a company of false prophets and one true one. If we read these stories carefully, we shall see what made some prophets false and others true. We shall note, also, why we consider the false prophets as fortune tellers and why we think of the true prophets as "God's angry men."

Saul and a "Company of Prophets"

The first story is of Saul, the farmer's son who became the first King of Israel.[1]

One day, back in the year 1028 B.C.E.,[2] a farmer of the tribe of Benjamin, in the southern part of Canaan, sent his son on an errand. Some donkeys had strayed away, and seemed to have been lost. He asked his son Saul — a tall, lanky teen-ager, probably red-headed and freckled — to find them. Saul took a young boy with him and set off in search of the beasts. It was wild, hilly and rocky country. The two roamed quite a ways for several days, but saw no sign of the animals. Saul thought it was time they returned home; his father must be worrying about him now even more than about

[1] I Sam. 10
[2] How long ago was it?

the donkeys. The young boy thought of a scheme. There was a famous old man in the region by the name of Samuel. He was popular throughout the country as an itinerant judge, priest, politician. He might be able to tell them where the animals might be found; prophets and priests of a certain kind knew such secret things the ordinary people did not know, he believed. Just then some peasant girls came along, and Saul and his companion asked them where they might find Samuel. The girls told them where he was officiating in the neighborhood.[3]

Samuel was highly revered by the people throughout the country. He traveled from town to town, village to village, "judged" the people — that is, settled their disputes — officiated at the local sacrifices, preached to them on special occasions. But he had grown old and too tired to carry on his duties; his sons were not the men they should have been, and were not fit to succeed him. One day the people asked him to find the right man and anoint him King over them. It was at this time that Saul came along on his humble errand.

Samuel was very much impressed with Saul; he anointed him King there and then — the first King of Israel — much against Saul's own desire. What concerns us at this time is the "band of prophets" Saul met after he left Samuel, and especially how these prophets behaved.

Samuel told Saul to stop worrying about the beasts; they were found, he assured him, and to return home. On the way, by the Tomb of Rachel, he would meet some men, who would be kind to him, and, going further, he would come

[3] It was the same Samuel, who, as a young child, was brought to the Temple at Shiloh and left with the aged priest Eli, by his mother. You will find the story in I Sam. I ff.

upon some prophets. The Bible story gives us a good description how these prophets acted: [4]

After that thou shalt come to the hill of God, where is the garrison of the Philistines; and it shall come to pass, when thou art come thither to the city, that thou shalt meet a band of prophets coming down from the high place with a psaltery, and a timbrel, and a pipe, and a harp before them; and they will be prophesying. And the spirit of the Lord will come mightily upon thee, and thou shalt prophesy with them, and shalt be turned into another man.

And it was so, that when he had turned his back to go from Samuel, God gave him another heart; and all those signs came to pass that day.

And when they came thither to the hill, behold, a band of prophets met him; and the spirit of God came mightily upon him, and he prophesied among them.[5]

Notice that these prophets roamed the country the way gypsies do. There were many of them. The Bible speaks of "a company of prophets." This is true of all the false prophets: they moved about in large groups; the true prophets were lonely men, who lived and thought very much alone. They were alone even when they were in crowded cities.

Notice, further, that these prophets played musical instruments: the psaltery, tabret, pipe, harp. By playing these instruments, at a fast tempo, no doubt, they would whip themselves into excitement and frenzy. Then they "prophesied."

Just what they did was, probably, chanting, dancing, carrying on the way the American Indians did around a campfire to the beating of tom-toms, or what swooning teen-agers do at times when under the spell of a fast jazz band. They thought that "the spirit of the Lord" was upon them. Saul,

[4] I Sam. 10.5–6
[5] I Sam. 10.9–10

caught up in this frenzy, the Bible story reports, was "turned into another man." That is, he was no longer himself, no longer the sensible, quiet peasant young man; now he was dancing, chanting, slapping his thighs. Someone who knew him was amazed at such a change in him, and is reported to have said, "What? Saul too among the prophets?"

The true prophets never engaged in much emotionalism; they did not use musical instruments to get themselves excited; they did not rave and chant and carry on. They were highly thoughtful, serious men, given to meditation and prayer, pretty much in solitude. Heavy burdens rested on their hearts, and worries upon their minds.

These raving, chanting, dancing prophets were foretelling the future — foretelling the future the way gypsy fortune tellers do — and were paid for their services. The true prophets never received pay for their speaking.

Perhaps you have heard your parents, or some other adults, talk about fortune tellers. Their business is to predict what will happen. For that they are paid. Many people consult fortune tellers; it is a foolish practice, but, nevertheless, many do. Some people do it for the fun of it; others are more serious about it.

How does a fortune teller know what will happen?

She (usually it is a woman) will gaze into a crystal ball, or read the palms of the questioner's hands. The fortune tellers are supposed to have some mystic power ordinary people do not have. The truth is that they do not know, and have no facts to enable them to predict what will happen the next day or the next week, or month or year.

There are legitimate and honest ways of reading the future. A weather man, for example, will forecast the weather a day or several days ahead. He has certain facts to help him. He makes his predictions on the basis of what is known as "cause and effect." A physician will foretell how a certain disease will run its course, or how a certain medicine will produce certain results. Businessmen, by studying business situations, will predict what will happen in the business world. These, and others — engineers, social workers, political scientists and many others — think and speak in terms of "cause and effect." But, legitimate as their predictions may be, they will not be too sure of themselves. The false prophets were only fortune tellers, who had no basis whatever for their predictions except their supposed mystic powers. They told people mostly what the people wanted to hear, for a price.

The true prophets, as we shall read later, did predict certain events; but they did it on the basis of social and moral causes. If a city was corrupt, if a government neglected the poor and the needy, if treaties were made with bad countries, if judges were dishonest, they predicted that misery and revolution would come upon the land. In this sense they did predict the future. We shall hear them say, over and over again: "It shall come to pass," and, "Thus saith the Lord." — predicting that this or that would happen if the people and their kings and priests persisted in their bad ways.

What we learn of these false prophets from the story of Saul, and from many other stories in the Bible, is, *first*, that they moved in gangs; *second*, that they would whip themselves into violent excitement by playing musical instruments; *third*, they foretold the future the way gypsy fortune tellers do — for a fee, without any factual basis or good logic for their predictions. The true prophets, we shall see, differed from them on all these points.

Nathan and "Thou Art the Man."

Our second story reports how a true prophet acted in a certain situation where brave speaking was highly dangerous but badly needed.

King David was a powerful monarch. He did pretty much as he pleased; there were few, if any, who dared oppose him.

Uriah was a faithful soldier in the King's army, who deserved well at David's hands. He had a beautiful wife, called Bath Sheba. David fell in love with her. He thought of a shameful way to get rid of her husband. A small war was in progress at that time. King David "promoted" Uriah to an especially dangerous outpost.

Uriah was killed; David had his Bath Sheba.

Word of this reached the prophet Nathan. We know hardly anything of this brave prophet. This we do know: he was furiously angry over David's disgraceful conduct. Ignoring all danger to himself, he presented himself at the royal palace, and told the young king the following story:

And the Lord sent Nathan unto David. And he came unto him, and said unto him: 'There were two men in one city: the one rich, and the other poor. The rich man had exceeding many flocks and herds; but the poor man had nothing, save one little ewe lamb, which he had bought and reared; and it grew up together with him, and with his children; it did eat of his own morsel, and drank of his own cup, and lay in his bosom, and was unto him as a daughter. And there came a traveller unto the rich man, and he spared to take of his own flock and of his own herd, to dress for the wayfaring man that was come unto him, but took the poor man's lamb, and dressed it for the man that was come to him.' And David's anger was greatly kindled against the man; and he said to Nathan: 'As the Lord liveth, the man that hath done this deserveth to die;

and he shall restore the lamb fourfold, because he did this thing, and because he had no pity.'

And Nathan said to David: 'Thou art the man.' [6]

Notice, first, that it took a great deal of courage for Nathan to face his king, who was an absolute monarch, and who might have beheaded him for such interference in his private life. Notice, further, that Nathan acted alone; he did not come with a gang of prophets. Notice, also, what it was that made Nathan so furiously angry: an injustice was committed.

The prophet did not play safe, he did not say to himself that his speaking to the popular king would make him unpopular at court and endanger him with David's friends generally. His own safety and his own popularity mattered not at all; it never entered his mind. He never said to himself: "This is none of my business." He felt outraged at such indecent conduct and announced himself as sent by God: "Thus saith the Lord."

Wherever and whenever a wrong was done, there the prophet appeared, boldly and defiantly, as the messenger of God. "The Lord hath sent me." They were sure that they communicated God's will. Their consciences would not permit them to play safe and keep quiet. [7]

Micaiah and the Word of God

In the third story we see how a gang of fortune telling prophets and one lone true prophet acted in a serious situation.

---

[6] II Sam. 12.1–8

[7] Read the story of Naboth's Vineyard in I Kings 21, and note how the prophet Elijah rebuked King Ahab, the way Nathan rebuked David, and how Elijah too said "Thus saith the Lord."

The kings of Israel and of Judah [8] entered into a partnership to attack a third state, Syria, and to capture a city, which, they claimed, belonged to Israel. That is, they were starting a war, for no good reason. The King of Judah was a bit in doubt, evidently; he thought they should first consult a prophet and find out what chances they had of winning the war. Then comes our story:

Then the king of Israel gathered the prophets together, about four hundred men, and said unto them: 'Shall I go against Ramothgilead to battle, or shall I forbear?' And they said: 'Go up; for the Lord will deliver it into the hand of the king.'

But Jehoshaphat (that is, the King of Judah) said: 'Is there not here besides a prophet of the Lord, that we might inquire of him?'

And the king of Israel said unto Jehoshaphat: 'There is yet one man by whom we might inquire of the Lord, Micaiah the son of Imlah; but I hate him; for he doth not prophesy good concerning me, but evil.' And Jehoshaphat said: 'Let not the king say so.'

Then the king of Israel called an officer, and said: 'Fetch quickly Micaiah the son of Imlah.'

Now the king of Israel and Jehoshaphat the king of Judah sat each on his throne, arrayed in their robes, in a threshing-floor, at the entrance of the gate of Samaria; and all the prophets prophesied before them.

And Zedekiah the son of Chenaanah made him horns of iron, and said: 'Thus saith the Lord: With these shalt thou gore the Arameans, until they be consumed.'

And all the prophets prophesied so, saying: 'Go up to Ramothgilead, and prosper; for the Lord will deliver it into the hand of the king.' [9]

[8] There were two Hebrew states after the death of King Solomon in the year 933 B.C.E. The north was Israel, consisting of ten tribes; the south was Judah, consisting of two tribes.
[9] I K. 22.6–12

These "four hundred" must have been dancing violently, howling, slapping their thighs, like Indians on the war path. Notice how their leader, Zedekiah, made himself "horns of iron," to render himself more fierce.

Meantime, the story continues:

> And the messenger that went to call Micaiah spoke unto him, saying 'Behold now, the words of the prophets declare good unto the king with one mouth, let thy word, I pray thee, be like the word of one of them, speak thou good.'
> And Micaiah said: 'As the Lord liveth, what the Lord saith unto me, that will I speak.' . . .
> And the king of Israel said to Jehoshaphat: 'Did I not tell thee that he would not prophesy good concerning me, but evil?' [10]

The false prophets were not concerned at all with the right or wrong of the situation. War is the greatest crime in history; it kills innocent men, women and children, and destroys cities and countries. But the false prophets were a howling mob, goading two stupid kings on a criminal adventure: "Go up and conquer!" They even added that the Lord had assured them that they would be victorious.

The true prophets denounced war as criminal.

As in the story of Saul, the prophets here too roam the countryside in large numbers, some four hundred of them! They told the kings what the kings wanted to hear. They were playing for popularity and a fat fee. Micaiah ben Imlah, true prophet that he was, would not follow the crowd. He was alone; he thought alone and had the courage to speak what he truly believed. " What the Lord saith unto me, that only will I speak."

[10] I K. 22. 13–14, 18.

TOPICS FOR FURTHER STUDY AND DISCUSSION

1. Look up the word "prophet" in a large dictionary. Does this definition apply to the false or the true prophets, or to both? How?

2. List the points of difference between the false and true prophets. Which of these points do you consider the most important?

3. Have you ever consulted a fortune teller? What did she predict? Did you believe her?

4. Can you write a script for a television performance of any of the stories given in this chapter? Try.

5. Are there prophets in the world today? Who? What makes you think of these men as prophets?

2. IDOLATRY

THE Hebrew prophets stormed furiously against idolatry. They used their angriest words in denouncing the false gods. To understand why they were so violently angry about idol worship, we must know what idolatry was like, what it meant.

Idolatry is the worship of idols; an idol is anything in place of God. The prophets speak of them as "no-gods," "things of nought," "detestations," "abominations." In that they were true spokesmen of the religion of Israel.

The second commandment demands:

Thou shalt have no other gods before me . . .
Thou shalt not make unto thee a graven image, nor any manner of likeness of anything that is in heaven above, or that is in the earth beneath, or that is in the water under the earth . . .[1]

Abraham, according to the rabbinic legend, smashed his father's idols in the open market place and chose to be the champion of the One God, Who made heaven and earth. You remember the story of the Golden Calf the Israelites in the desert made while Moses was away on Mount Sinai. They made it of gold and all sorts of jewelry, danced around it and chanted in excitement, "This is your God, O Israel." This sin brought much sorrow upon Moses and "the generation of the desert."

[1] Exod. 20.3–4; Deut. 5.7–9

Elijah

One of the great stories in the Bible is how the prophet Elijah challenged the false prophets and their idols.[2] This is one of the many stories and legends told of Elijah by the people who admired him for his zeal and his courage.

Elijah criticized his king, Ahab, and, especially, the queen, Jezebel, who encouraged the people in their idolatrous practices. At one time he had to flee for his life. One day King Ahab and Elijah met. There was violent feeling between them. Once again, as in the cases of Nathan and Micaiah ben Imlah, we see the courage of the lone prophet in attacking evil. The Bible reports:

And it came to pass, when Ahab saw Elijah, that Ahab said unto him: 'Is it thou, thou troubler of Israel?'
And he answered: 'I have not troubled Israel; but thou, and thy father's house, in that ye have forsaken the commandments of the Lord, and thou hast followed the Baalim.

Elijah challenged Ahab's hundreds of prophets to a contest. The author who wrote this story, and perhaps also the editors who, later, revised it, enlarged on it, the way any good story teller or playwright does to make the story or play more exciting.

And Ahab sent unto all the children of Israel, and gathered the prophets together unto Mount Carmel. And Elijah came near unto all the people, and said: 'How long halt ye between two opinions? if the Lord be God, follow Him: but if Baal, follow him.' And the people answered him not a word. Then said Elijah unto the people: 'I, even I only, am left a prophet of the

[2] I K. 18.17–28

Lord; but Baal's prophets are four hundred and fifty men. Let them therefore give us two bullocks; and let them choose one bullock for themselves, and cut it in pieces, and lay it on the wood, and put no fire under; and I will dress the other bullock, and lay it on the wood, and put no fire under. And call ye on the name of your god, and I will call on the name of the Lord; and the God that answereth by fire, let him be God.' And all the people answered and said: 'It is well spoken.'

The author invents some humor, to make his story more interesting. He ridicules the dim-witted idolators:

And it came to pass at noon, that Elijah mocked them, and said: 'Cry aloud; for he is a god; either he is musing, or he is gone aside, or he is in a journey, or peradventure he sleepeth, and must be awaked.' And they cried aloud, and cut themselves after their manner with swords and lances, till the blood gushed out upon them.

Here we see again how the false prophets behaved while they were prophesying — dancing, chanting, throwing themselves about violently.

The story ends with Elijah's triumph over the false prophets, but he had to flee from the wrath of King Ahab. He took shelter in a cave. Here is another legend told of Elijah by a later author. It is in this story that we have the most famous of all passages in the Bible describing how God spoke to the prophets, and how He speaks to us and all people everywhere:

And he came thither unto a cave, and lodged there; and, behold, the word of the Lord came to him, and He said unto him: 'What doest thou here, Elijah?' And he said: 'I have been very jealous for the Lord, the God of hosts; for the children of Israel have forsaken Thy covenant, thrown down Thine altars, and slain Thy prophets with the sword; and I even I only, am left; and they seek

my life, to take it away.' And He said: 'Go forth, and stand upon
the mount before the Lord.'   And, behold, the Lord passed by,
and a great and strong wind rent the mountains, and broke in
pieces the rocks before the Lord; but the Lord was not in the
wind; and after the wind an earthquake; but the Lord was not in
the earthquake; and after the earthquake a fire; but the Lord was
not in the fire; and after the fire a still small voice.[3]

In the book of Isaiah we have one of the most sarcastic
passages ridiculing the smug stupidity of the idol maker.

A man selects a log.   Part of it he uses for fuel and of the
left-over he makes a little god, in the shape of a man.   He
roasts meat over the fire, gorges himself, pats his fat belly and
feels smug and satisfied with himself:

> He burneth half thereof in the fire;
> With half thereof he eateth flesh;
> He roasteth roast, and is satisfied;
> Yea, he warmeth himself, and saith:
> 'Aha! I am warm . . .'
> And of the left-over he maketh a god, even his graven image;
> He falleth down unto it and worshippeth,
> And prayeth unto it,
> And saith: 'Deliver me, for thou art my god!' [4]

Ba'alim and "the Hosts of Heaven"

An idol is more — a great deal more — than a mere toy, or
a little figure on a mantle piece, or a statue, or a carving on a
totem pole.   Were idols only these, they would be stupid
enough, but not important enough to rouse the anger of the
prophets.   Idols had to do with ugly and immoral behavior,
and even with life and death.   They corrupted people.

[3] I K. 19.10–12
[4] Isaiah 44.16–17

When the Israelites, following Moses, came into Canaan, under the leadership of Joshua, they found the land inhabited by many people. Each of these tribes and nations had its own gods and goddesses, its own idol-worship. The country-side was filled with shrines, and each shrine was a center of idol worship. In the book of Deuteronomy we are told how the lawgivers who followed the teachings of Moses tried to rid the land of "all these abominations."

One group of gods was known as *ba'alim. Ba'al* means master, owner, or possessor. These spirits were believed to have possessed certain places or objects. Thus there were the ba'al of trees, of mountains, of wells, of fields, of great rocks. These trees and mountains and wells, fields and rocks and trees, were like haunted houses. A spirit dwelt in them and possessed them. No one might touch them or use them unless the god or spirit was satisfied, and to make these spirits friendly and kindly disposed, sacrifices had to be offered to them. If a tree withered and bore no fruit, if a well went dry, if a field would not yield a harvest, the *ba'alim* were believed to be angry. To win their cooperation and good will, gifts were brought to the sanctuary, animals were sacrificed upon the altars. Most horrible of all, even infant boys – the first born – were sacrificed and their blood smeared on the altar.

In addition to the ba'alim – that is the spirits – there were other gods, vicious and evil deities. There were, for example, *Ashtoreth*, the goddess who was believed to have controlled human birth; *Moloch*, who demanded that the first-born boys be sacrificed to him. That is why we speak of Moloch as the god of war. The English poet Milton, in his poem, *Paradise Lost*, speaks of this horrible deity as follows:

> Moloch, horrid king, besmeared with blood
> Of human sacrifice and parent's tears.

Some of our biblical ancestors, on settling in Canaan, took to worshipping these deities. They did what their Canaanitish neighbors did, despite the laws of Moses, which forbid this horrible practice. Mosaic law even requires capital punishment for any man who sacrifices a son to the deities.

A tragic story of human sacrifice in ancient Israel is told in the book of Judges.[5]

Jephtah's Daughter

Jephtah was a tribal warrior. He was set for battle with some enemy tribes. Before plunging into warfare he made a rash vow: he would, if he were victorious, sacrifice any living thing which came out of his house to meet him on his way from battle.

And Jephthah came to Mizpah unto his house, and behold, his daughter came out to meet him with timbrels and with dances; and she was his only child; beside her he had neither son nor daughter. And it came to pass, when he saw her, that he rent his clothes, and said: 'Alas, my daughter! thou hast brought me very low, and thou art become my troubler; for I have opened my mouth unto the Lord, and I cannot go back.'

The story continues:

And he did with her as he had vowed.[6]

[5] Read up on *ba'al Ashtoreth,* (or *Ishtar, Ashtarte*) *Moloch, Milkom,* etc. in any good encyclopedia. You will find the stories of these deities interesting.
[6] Judges 11.34–35

The Idols Outlawed

One of the greatest gifts the Hebrew prophets made to us and to all mankind was their merciless attacks on this barbaric practice and finally discrediting it. We shall read more on this point as we progress in our study of the prophets.

Because idols were so much more than mere toys, or statues, and idolatry meant practicing not only innocent foolishness but engaging in evil practices, the Rabbis of the Talmud followed the teachings of the prophets and declared that idol worship meant violating all the commandments of the Torah. "He who commits idolatry," they said, "denies the Ten Commandments." They could think of no worse sin than idolatry.

TOPICS FOR FURTHER STUDY AND DISCUSSION

1. Have you ever been in a "haunted house" or have you read any stories of haunted houses?
   What makes the house haunted?
2. Write a script for a television performance of Elijah and the false prophets on Mount Carmel.
3. Are we worshipping idols today?
   Explain. Are cities or countries worshipping idols? Explain.
4. Are we offering human sacrifices today?
5. Do you agree with the Talmudic masters that he who commits idolatry violates all the Ten Commandments? Explain.

3. AMOS

Let justice well up as waters,
And righteousness as a mighty stream (Amos 5.24)

Literary Prophets

OUR first literary prophet is Amos. By a "literary" prophet
we mean a prophet who wrote a book, or whose name is
associated with a book. Nathan, Micaiah ben Imlah, Elijah
are not counted among the literary prophets for the reason
that no books have come down to us in their names. In Jewish tradition Moses is considered the chief of the prophets;
but we today consider him as the chief lawgiver rather than
prophet. Moses gave us laws and commandments, whereas
the prophets left us their visions and teachings in the form
of sermons or orations.

Amos at Beth-El

Imagine the Temple at Beth-El in northern Israel in the
year 750 B.C.E. We do not know how the Temple was laid
out. But, we do know that it was a famous and rich temple,
perhaps the richest sanctuary in the country. It must have
been a most imposing building. In design, appointments, and
kind of worship it had no relation to ours at all. At this par-
ticular time it was crowded with people, come from all parts
of the country. It may have been a holiday. The king himself was there; the queen must have been there; the military

men — generals, captains and soldirs — were there. Of course, the priests were there, officiating at the altar; the musicians were there intoning the service. The people had brought offerings — perhaps first fruits of the harvest, or early grain, or even animals for sacrifice. Beth-El, literally "house of God," was a happy, rich, proud congregation keeping holiday.

Suddenly an angry voice rose above the hubbub, the chanting and general excitement. Someone was saying terrible things about the rich exploiting the poor, the corrupt judges, the ignorant priests, the arrogant military men. The country, this voice continued, would be conquered by a cruel enemy and all these proud people would be killed or led away as war prisoners into a barbaric land. The people were amazed and listened, fascinated.

Who was this man who was saying such terrible things? He spoke in a Judean accent, the language of the southern part of the country. His dress too — probably the same as worn by Bedouins to-day — must have been out of place in such a formal place and time as the service at the temple, where all the fashionable men and women were gathered. Angry words were pouring out of his mouth like a torrent. He was saying astonishing things. Who was this uninvited, unannounced, rustic preacher?

Life in Tekoa

His name was Amos, who was "among the herdsmen of Tekoa." Tekoa was a settlement some fifteen miles south of Jerusalem. Today this general area is the beginning of the Negev, the southland. The Bible describes it as "a waste and howling wilderness." Very little of anything could grow there, only patches of poor wheat and poor grazing spots. Rocks upon rocks and rolling hills of rocks, with only some brownish green patches, could be seen. Limestone hills were in the distance; beyond, to the south was Moab, to the east the land dropped downward toward the Dead Sea, where nothing grew. On a clear day Amos could see the towers of Jerusalem on the horizon to the north. Lack of water was the constant problem; wells were fiercely guarded, for they meant life or death for man and beast. The days were mercilessly hot, the temperature rising well above a hundred degrees, and no shadows to afford shelter; the nights were cold. Wild, starved beasts prowled, searching for prey. But the moon and the stars shone all the brighter; the skies were infinite, as far as the eyes could see.

A shepherd in such a country must be alert, or he and his flock perish in one night.

Amos heard the roaring of the lion shattering the stillness of the night; he heard the cries of the prey. He must have watched the brilliant moon and stars in the infinite heavens above him; he saw shooting stars cutting the vast, endless heavens, like lightning, and thought of God beyond.

He was a shepherd. The sheep he tended were black, short, squatty little beasts, prized for their wool. He was, also, the Bible informs us, "a dresser of sycamores" — small fruit, something like a small fig. They were not very tasty, but in such a country food is scarce and every kind of food is carefully preserved.

There seems to have been a settlement of shepherds at or near Tekoa. Travelers would come through the country from time to time, on the way to Egypt, to sell their wares or to buy. Amos, no doubt, met them, talked with them of the life in the cities; he heard their reports of how the rich were exploiting the poor, of the cruel taxation imposed by the King and his generals on the helpless weak, of the arrogance of the powerful, of the corrupt judges who were using the courts to their own selfish advantage; he must have heard a good deal of the neglect of the poor, the sick, the widows and the orphans. He brooded over these evils and was sure that the punishments of God would fall upon the sinful land. That is why he spoke as he did at Beth-El.

Amos Preaches

We return to Beth-El and listen to Amos's angry sermon.

He began with a furious denunciation of the countries roundabout Judah. They were gangster nations. They robbed, killed and showed no mercy; they enlarged their borders, extended their own power by plundering their neighbors. They sold human beings into slavery. They grew rich on the broken bodies of innocent men and women. They were savage, brutal; therefore, he thundered, the punishments of God would fall upon them. Their cities would be reduced to heaps of ruins, their palaces would be burned down to the ground; proud, haughty people to-day, tomorrow they would be led off in chains as war prisoners.

The people listened in astonishment as Amos spoke these terrible words in the name of God. "Hear ye this word," he went on, denouncing one country after another — Syria, Philistia, Phoenicia, Edom, Ammon, Moab. The Judeans at Beth-El were probably pleased, and even amused. They hated these countries that surrounded them, and enjoyed hearing of evil things befalling them.

But, after attacking all the neighboring countries, he attacked Judah. The Judeans were guilty of oppressing the poor and robbing the needy. A poor man had no chance in the courts, he was sold for a mere trinket. Still, the royalty, the military, the priest, the aristocratic and self-satisfied women listened, pleased and amused. Amos was brilliant in capturing and holding their attention.

Then he shifted his fire to Israel and the people right there before him, their temple, their sacrifices, their chanting.

Judah and Israel were two sister states. The north, Israel, seceded from the south, Judah, under the leadership of Jereboam after the death of Solomon (933 B.C.E.) Though both were Hebrew states, each following, presumably, the laws of Moses, both the children of Abraham, Isaac and Jacob, they, nevertheless, hated each other — the way the North and the South in our own American Civil War fought and hated each other. Amos refused to see any difference between them. He considered them one country and spoke of them as "the whole family" whom God had liberated from Egypt.

Turning to the astonished men and women before him, he continued his angry sermon, and the people listened:

Hear ye this word . . .
You who turn justice to poison
And cast righteousness to the ground . . .
Because you trample upon the poor,
And take exactions of wheat from them *
Though you have built houses of hewn stones **
You shall not dwell in them,
Though you have planted pleasant vineyards
You shall not drink the wine thereof.

* That is, rob them of their daily bread.
** That is, grand palaces.

For I know how manifold are your crimes,
And how mighty are your sins —
You that browbeat the righteous, take bribes,
And defeat the poor in the gate.***
Seek good and not evil, that you may live,
And so the Lord, the God of hosts, may be with you, as you say;
Hate evil and love the good;
Set justice on her feet again in the courts.
Perhaps the Lord God will have mercy upon you . . .[1]

Amaziah Interrupts

The chief priest at Beth-El was a man by the name of Amaziah. He listened in astonishment, and then interrupted Amos; he could stand such talk no longer. Treason! he cried. "The land is not able to bear all his words. . . . O thou seer,[2] go! Flee into the land of Judah and there prophesy, but prophesy not again here at Beth-El, for it is the King's chapel and a royal sanctuary."[3] What Amaziah was saying was: You, Amos, dressed in your shepherd's clothes and speaking in a foreign accent, go back where you came from and there talk, but not here. This is the King's own Temple!

But Amos did not flee. He remained and spoke his mind. He addressed himself particularly to the smug and sleek men and women before him. "Hear ye this word," he continued in the name of God:

I hate, I despise your feasts,
And I will take no delight in your solemn assemblies.
Yea, though you offer me burnt offerings and your meal offerings,
I will not accept them;

*** That is, at court.
[1] 5 (selected verses)
[2] *Seer* was the older word for prophet.
[3] Amos 7.12

Neither will I regard the meal offerings of your fat beasts.
Take away from me the noise of your songs;
And let me not hear the melodies of your psalteries.
But let justice well up as waters,
And righteousness as a mighty stream.[4]

Amos, and the prophets who followed him, punctured
many conceits the people cherished. Their religious observances, he told them, were hateful to God. What God wanted
was justice, not sacrifices, not incantations. Their prosperity
and their glamor would go up in smoke before the invaders,
and the proud and pampered ladies would be disgraced and
dragged into captivity.

The Chosen People and the Day of the Lord

Two further national conceits Amos attacked in anger.

The people — from the king, the military, the priests, down
to the masses — believed they were God's special people, the
Chosen People, chosen by Him for special privilege. That
was a bad conceit. Yes, God did bring Israel out of Egypt,
but not because God played favorites. It was an act of justice. He had liberated other peoples too.

> Are ye not as the children of the Ethiopians unto Me,
> O children of Israel? saith the Lord.
> Have not I brought up Israel out of the land of Egypt,
> And the Philistines from Caphtor,
> And Aram from Kir? [5]

The Ethiopians were a Negroid people; but God knows no
color line. When a judge finds a case in favor of one party

[4] 5.21–24
[5] 9.7

rather than the other, it is not because he favors or likes one party better than the other. He follows the dictates of justice, not of personal favoritism.

Being God's chosen people does not mean being chosen for special privilege. What it does mean is that special responsibilities rest upon the people who make the claim to being chosen; they must be worthy of such high distinction.

> You only have I known of all the families of the earth;
> Therefore I will visit upon you all your iniquities.[6]

A people that had been liberated from slavery, must know better and understand more deeply the oppressed of the earth. A people that had stood at Sinai and accepted the Law must be a just and honorable people.

Thus Amos accepted the belief of the Chosen People, but he scorned the easy and cheap interpretation of it. Instead, he gave its prophetic meaning: Being God's people means doing God's will in the world.[*]

The people believed, also, in what was known as the Day of the Lord. A day would come when Israel would triumph over all the other peoples. All the enemies would be humbled; Israel would be gloriously victorious. Israel's God would vindicate them.

Again Amos accepts the belief held by the people, but he gave it a prophetic meaning. Yes, the Day of the Lord will come; but it will not be a day of triumph and exaltation over all the surrounding peoples. Instead, it will be a day of judg-

---

[6] 3.2

[*] Do people who hold great offices — the President of the United States, the Governor of the State, the head of a university, the judge, the physician, the teacher, the rabbi, or men of great wealth, have special obligations *because* of the positions they hold?

ment. Israel will stand before the bar of divine justice, and a just God will pronounce sentence — not in keeping with favoritism for any one nation, but in keeping with the eternal justice which God wants to prevail in the world. It is only national arrogance and national conceit that made the Israelites expect glorious victories.[7]

The Plumbline

This is the heart of Amos. God wants justice — justice between man and man, justice between country and country. That is the only kind of religion God wants of man, Amos argued.

He concluded his sermon with several "visions." * These make one point: the country would fall before the enemy. That is God's punishment of a sinful nation, the punishment for social injustice.

One of these visions is that of a mason building a wall. He watches a plumbline as he lays brick upon brick, to see if he is building it straight. To Amos' imagination that is the way God builds the good society. The plumbline is justice. If a city, or a country, is built according to the plumbline of justice, it will be strong and will endure, and the people will be secure; but if the city or country is crooked, it will collapse.

What happened to Amos after he finished speaking we do not know. He must have gone back to Tekoa, its heat and cold, his stunted little black sheep and his short sycamore trees, and heard the roaring of the hungry lions and the cries of their prey; he, no doubt, shielded his flock, watched the moon high

[7] 5.18–20
* Look up "vision" in a good dictionary. What does it mean as Amos uses it?

in the sky, watched the stars and the shooting meteors, and brooded of God beyond and the terrible need for justice among men.

TOPICS FOR FURTHER STUDY AND DISCUSSION

1. Look up the Negev on a map of present-day Israel. Reproduce this country on your map. What crops are grown there now? What major problems have the settlers to overcome? How do these compare with the situation in the days of Amos?

2. Paraphrase, in your own words, the selections from Amos given in this chapter. Was Amos opposed to formal religion?

3. Write a play for television on Amos and Amaziah.

4. Explain the concept of "the Chosen People" as held by the Judeans and as interpreted by Amos. Should Jews today consider themselves a Chosen People? Explain.

    Do you believe that Jews today should drop from their prayer-book the blessing spoken before reading from the Torah: "Blessed be Thou, Lord our God, King of the Universe, Who has chosen us from among all peoples and hast given us Thy Torah?" Explain. See the translation in the Union Prayer Book, pages 145–6.

    Have other peoples considered themselves Chosen People? Which people? In what sense of the term?

5. Explain the idea of the Day of the Lord as held by the Judeans and as interpreted by Amos.

    Have other peoples in history believed in a Day of the Lord, when they would triumph over all other countries? Explain.

6. Write a speech for Amos which he would deliver before the United Nations.

7. Would you like to have Amos as your personal friend, to visit with you, and go on trips with you — say to the South where we have trouble in race relations, or to Las Vegas, where there is a great deal of gambling? What would Amos be talking about and what would he be saying?

4. HOSEA

I will betroth thee unto Me forever;
Yea, I will betroth thee unto Me in righteousness and justice,
And in lovingkindness and in compassion;
I will betroth thee unto Me in faithfulness,
And thou shalt know the Lord. (Hosea 2.21–22)

A Prophet's Marriage

ABOUT fifteen years after Amos preached his sermon at Beth-El, another prophet began to speak, in the manner of all the Hebrew prophets: protesting against the injustices, the cruelties, the crimes, the idolatries of the people, and calling on them, in the name of God, to change their ways. His name was Hosea. Unlike Amos, and all the other prophets, who were Judeans, Hosea came from northern Israel.

He was a man of great sorrow. He had a tragic family life. We are told about it in chapters 1 and 3 of his book. The story is not very clear in detail, but the two chapters do agree that he had a terribly unhappy marriage.

He loved his wife deeply, but she was unfaithful and betrayed his love. Her name was Gomer; the Bible refers to her as Gomer-not-worth-a-fig — as we would say, Gomer-not-worth-two-cents. Three children were born to them, two sons and one daughter. He gave them strange names. His first-born son he called Jezreel; his second, a daughter, he called Lo-ruhamah; his third, a boy, he named Lo-ammi.

Why such strange names? Because his own tragic family

life made him think of the tragic condition of the country. These names are his way of telling the people what he was most anxious for them to understand. He spoke in a parable; his children were living sermons.[1]

The Parable

God, like Hosea, loved Israel deeply. He liberated them from Egypt and brought them to "a land flowing with milk and honey." He expected Israel to be worthy of His great love — that is, to be a just, faithful people, living by the commandments of Moses. Instead, Israel went bad. There were special reasons for it.

Between the time of Amos at Beth-El and Hosea many developments had taken place in Israel and much distress came upon the land.

King Jereboam II died in 749 B.C.E. and political anarchy followed. In some dozen years four kings were assassinated. A fifth king was captured in battle. That meant dreadful and constant upheavals. The country, under a weak king by the name of Menahem, paid heavy tribute to the Assyrians who had overrun the land. That meant heavy taxation on the people. The poor, as always under such circumstances, suffered most. The warnings Amos had spoken were coming true.

Large cities had sprung up (large, that is, for their time; not so large by our standards.) Trade routes between Egypt to the southwest and Babylonia, Phoenicia, Arabia to the northeast passed through the rich agricultural valleys of Israel. Many grew wealthy; but the peasants and small farmers

[1] Look up the word *parable* in a good dictionary.

were crowded out. Large landholders increased their estates; the small farmers were losing their meager holdings. With large centers of population came special problems: unemployment, a landless peasantry, poverty, crime. Governments had not yet learned how to control these evils. Still more, they had not yet learned the need to control them. The prophets had not yet built up a strong social conscience.

Hosea gives us a terrible picture of social evils: robbery, perjury, lying, drunkenness, corrupt judges, greedy priests, superstitious people. Every one, he laments, is concerned with his own good times and nothing more.

The people of Israel went after "the strange gods." They imitated their pagan neighbors, and worshipped the *ba'alim*, Chemosh, Ashtoreth, Moloch, which we described in our chapter on Idolatry. "Israel is stubborn like a stubborn heifer," Hosea complains, wedded to idols.

"The Lord hath a controversy with His people," the way Hosea had with his faithless Gomer.

Hear the word of the Lord, ye children of Israel!
For the Lord hath a controversy with the inhabitants of the land,
Because there is no truth, nor mercy,
Nor knowledge of God in the land.
(There is nothing but) perjury and lying, and robbery, and murder, and adultery, and constant violence and bloodshed.[2]

Their priests are just as bad as the people. "Like people like priest," the prophet complains sadly. They do not teach people what is right and do not set the right example. "My people are destroyed for lack of knowledge," and "a people that is without understanding must come to ruin." [3]

[2] 4.1–2
[3] 11,14

He pleaded with his people to reform and live, the way he pleaded with his wife to change her ways and continue their life together honorably as husband and wife. That is why he gave his children such fantastic names: they were warnings. Jezreel meant final defeat. The name had the same meaning to the people that Gettysburg had to the South in our American Civil War. Lo-ruhamah meant "no-mercy"; Lo-ammi meant, "not my people"; that is, defeat, or destruction, no mercy and final rejection.

A Door of Hope

How might Hosea get his wife to change her ways? How might God get his people Israel to change their ways?

First, Hosea might punish Gomer; second, he might divorce her; third, he might try to change her with "compassion and tender mercy." The first two ways were the easy ones, and might have solved the problem for Hosea; it would not have solved the problem for Gomer, but the evil would have remained. Hosea chose the hard way, but the most deeply religious. He would transform the evil into good. He chose the way of *hesed*, loving kindness, deep, patient love and compassion. As we today would express it, Gomer was a sick woman. We cannot beat emotionally sick people into mental health. It takes enormous patience, tender mercy, infinite love. Hosea felt what the psychiatrists in our time know and practice — understanding, patience, love.

That is the way God deals with Israel. God's infinite love will heal and redeem the sinful people; but the people must do their full share, must understand their own shortcomings, must be willing to be helped. People who are not willing to be

helped in their emotional troubles, the psychiatrists tell us, cannot be helped at all by any one.

Hosea pleaded with his people to "return to the Lord." That was his way of saying, change your ways, give up the false gods and live. In the language of our parable, God is the husband speaking to his beloved, Israel:

> I will betroth thee unto Me forever;
> Yea, I will betroth thee unto Me in righteousness and justice,
> And in lovingkindness and in compassion;
> I will betroth thee unto Me in faithfulness,
> And thou shalt know the Lord.[4]

TOPICS FOR FURTHER STUDY AND DISCUSSION

1. Memorize the text under the title of this chapter.
   What do these words mean: *betroth, lovingkindness, compassion, know the Lord.*
2. Which of the two prophets do you like better, Amos or Hosea? Why?
3. On your map indicate the trade routes between Egypt and Phoenicia, Babylon, Arabia.
4. State the problems that developed in Israel between the days of Amos and Hosea. What would we in our time be doing about these? What was done during the days of Hosea?
5. Were Hosea alive today, what profession would he be likely to follow: physician? lawyer? rabbi? psychiatrist? Which of these professions would Amos be likely to follow?
6. What is meant by "social conscience"? "social justice"? Give examples a) from Hosea; b) from our time.

[4] 2.21–22

5. ISAIAH

Holy, holy, holy is the Lord of hosts;
The whole earth is full of his glory. (Isaiah 6.3)

ISAIAH was a young boy in Jerusalem when Amos preached
his sermon at Beth-El in Israel; he was in his teens when Hosea
pleaded for loving kindness in man's dealings with his fellow
man. About the year 740 B.C.E. he began to brood over his
duties as prophet of God.

He was a native of Jerusalem, and he loved the Holy City
passionately; but four times he saw his beloved "Judah and
Jerusalem" invaded by the enemy. Invasion meant fire and
plunder and murder, without pity. He saw his friends killed
and some of them deported by the invader. Isaiah's heart was
heavy with grief.

Let us join Isaiah on his way to the Temple in Jerusalem
about the year 740 B.C.E. He was deeply distressed. Alarms
of war were sweeping the land; fear was freezing the hearts
of men and women. His own King, Ahaz, was distressed and
confused and did not know which way to turn for help.
Isaiah was convinced that the King was making a wrong
decision; war would surely follow and the Holy City would
be reduced to rubble.

The sister state, Israel, to the north, and Syria, still farther
north, entered into an alliance to wage war against Assyria.[1]

[1] Syria and Assyria must not be confused. Syria was a small state north of
Israel; Assyria was a world empire to the north east, in Mesopotamia, in

Assyria was the terror of the world at that time. It had conquered state after state; deported most of the people who
were not butchered, appointed Assyrian governors over the
native populations that were left, and squeezed enormous taxes
from the poor people. The Assyrian armies, made up mainly
of barbaric recruits from everywhere, were heading toward
Syria and Israel. Next was Judah. The kings of Israel and
Syria were pressing King Ahaz of Judah to join them in a war
against Assyria. The King was hesitating, at a time when he
needed to be clear in his mind and firm in his policy. He
thought of appealing directly to the Assyrian King. Isaiah
thought that was inviting suicide; once the Assyrian cat was
taken into the Judean household it would quickly grow into a
tiger and devour the host.

Deeply worried, young Isaiah entered the Temple. We can
imagine him leaning against the doorpost, or wall, lost in
thought. Perhaps a thin column of smoke issued from a sacred
lamp on the altar; deep, dark shadows crowded the sanctuary.
Perhaps some light broke in from somewhere piercing these
shadows. Isaiah brooded. He was transported, carried away
in his imagination. He heard an angel choir; heard the rus-
tling of wings; heard the voice of God. He gives us a vivid
description of this awesome hour, which we consider as his
inauguration as prophet. Chapter 6 of the book of Isaiah
should be read as *imagery* — that is, highly poetic and imaginative; it must not be read as factual, no more than we read
Coleridge's *Ancient Mariner*, or Poe's *Raven*, literally.

---

the Tigris-Euphrates region. Assyria was the most powerful, plundering
world empire at the time of Isaiah. Examine a map of this period and note
the positions of: Israel, Judah, Syria, Assyria, Egypt. Notice that Judah
and Israel were battlefields between Egypt to the south west and Assyria
and later Babylon, and still later, Persia — to the north east.

Holy, holy, holy is the Lord of hosts;
The whole earth is full of His glory.
And the foundations of the thresholds were moved at the voice of
him that cried, and the house was filled with smoke. Then said I,
Woe is me! for I am undone;
Because I am a man of unclean lips,
And I dwell in the midst of a people of unclean lips;
For mine eyes have seen the King, the Lord of hosts.
Then flew one of the seraphim unto me, having a live coal in his
hands, which he had taken with tongs from off the altar. He
touched my mouth with it and said,
Lo, this hath touched thy lips;
And thine iniquity is taken away, and thy sin expiated.
And I heard the voice of the Lord saying,
Whom shall I send,
And who will go for us?
Then said I,
Here am I; send me.[2]

Life of Isaiah

Following the inaugural vision, which must have shaken
him badly, he began to speak his mind as prophet, speaking in
highly imaginative, poetic words. He is considered "the
prince of the prophets." Many scholars claim that he was
the greatest of all the prophets — greatest in his criticisms of
the evils of his time, in his advice to king and people, and, especially, in his impassioned poetic speeches and visions.

[2] Isaiah 6. *I am undone . . . for mine eyes have seen the King*. The belief was that instant death comes upon anyone who catches a glimpse of
God. That is why the angels described in this chapter use two of their
wings to cover their faces and eyes; even angels, according to this poem,
and Isaiah's imagination, must not see God. See Exod. 3.6 for a similar expression of this belief in the life of Moses.
Seraphim, supernatural creatures, like enormous birds with six wings, or angels. Isaiah is the only author in the Bible to use this term.

He was active for some forty years as prophet. We see him first in the year 735 B.C.E. or a year or two earlier, when he advised King Ahaz not to join in the alliance against Assyria. Later events showed that he was a wise counselor. He was married about the time he had the vision in the Temple, and had a son, who bore the strange name: *Maher-shalal-hash-baz*. Later he had another son, who too had a name queer to us: *Shear-jashub*. Like the prophet Hosea, Isaiah gave his children symbolic names; thereby he wanted to point a lesson to the people. The older boy's name meant: *Swift-booty-spoil-prey*. What he meant to tell the people was that the Assyrian armies were on the way to despoil, rob and plunder the land. The policies they and their king were following, he argued, would lead to disaster for the country. The second son's name meant: *A remnant will return.* Always Isaiah held up hope to the people, much more so than did Amos. Some — a few — people will be left, and they will be faithful and will, in the long run of history, save Judah. We speak of that as "a faithful remnant."

No one followed his advice, neither king nor people. For a time he retired from his speaking and advising. Meantime, enormous events were taking place. The most important was that Assyria invaded Israel and carried off "the Ten Lost Tribes," thus putting an end to the northern Kingdom of Israel forever, in the year 721 B.C.E.

Isaiah felt sure that "a faithful remnant" would in time save his people and his country, of which he usually spoke as "Judah and Jerusalem." He wrote down his prophecies, discouraged by the events of the time, but kept his faith in the future. In time, "in those days," a faithful remnant will return. Thus he "sealed his teachings among his disciples," and waited for the Lord.

The prophets did highly strange things to communicate their ideas to the people. We have noticed how Hosea and Isaiah gave their children symbolic names, to serve as living warnings. About the year 720 B.C.E., when Isaiah was well known as a prophet and adviser to the king, he walked about the streets of Jerusalem practically naked and barefoot, thus dramatizing to the people what would befall them if they involved themselves in the war with Assyria.

In the year 701 B.C.E. the Assyrian armies were encamped around Jerusalem. The Holy City was in a desperate situation. No one was permitted to come in nor to go out; famine and drought threatened the people. That night a fantastic thing happened; a plague swept through the Assyrian encampment. Most of the soldiers perished. The Assyrian general, Sennacherib, retreated. The people saw in that God's miraculous intervention.[3]

At about this time Isaiah disappeared from view. No man knows when or where he died. In round figures, therefore, we may say that he carried on as prophet between the years 740 to 701 B.C.E., a period of about forty years.

Song of the Vineyard

Isaiah was a patriot; he loved Jerusalem passionately. But he was not a blind patriot, not one to say, "My country is always right, all other countries are always wrong." He loved

---

[3] Is. 37.36–37. Lord Byron wrote his famous poem on this incident: "The Destruction of Sennacherib." Read it.

his country, and because he loved Judah, he was anxious to see Judah do the right thing and act honorably. One of his little speeches, in poetic form, criticizing his country, is known as The Song of the Vineyard.

Dressed as a minstrel, musical instrument in hand, he took his place one day when people were gathering their harvest and began chanting a ballad which he had composed:

> Let me sing of my well-beloved a song
> Of my beloved touching his vineyard.
> My well-beloved had a vineyard
> In a very fruitful hill;
> And he made a trench about it,
>   and gathered out the stones thereof,
> And planted it with the choicest vine,
> And built a tower in the midst of it,
> And also hewed out a wine vat therein;
> And he looked that it should bring forth grapes,
> And it brought forth wild grapes.
>
> And now, O inhabitants of Jerusalem,
> And men of Judah,
> Judge, I pray you, between me and my vineyard.
> What more could have been done for my vineyard,
> That I have not done for it?
> Wherefore, when I looked for it to yield grapes,
> Did it yield wild grapes?
>
> And now let me tell you, I pray,
> What I will do to my vineyard:
> I will take away the hedge thereof,
> And it shall be eaten up;
> And I will break down the fence thereof,
> And it shall be trodden down;
> And I will lay it waste;

It shall not be pruned nor hoed,
But there shall come up briers and thorns;
I will also command the clouds
That they rain no rain upon it.

The people who had gathered about him listened and were, no doubt, amused. They must have poked each other in the ribs and laughed delightedly, "That's true! That's true." Then Isaiah, abruptly, clinched his point:

For the vineyard of the Lord of hosts
    is the house of Israel,
And the men of Judah His pleasant plant:
And He looked for justice, but behold oppression;
For righteousnes, but behold a cry.[4]

The Wild Grapes of Judah

Then Isaiah went on to specify the sins of the cities. He must have repeated these charges over and over again, to king and people, who would or would not listen. He spoke of these evils as "the wild grapes of Judah." Wild grapes intoxicate people and make them sick. These wild grapes, he charged, were monopoly, the rich and the strong crowding out the poor and the weak; drunkenness — people get up early in the morning so that they may have more time for drinking intoxicating drinks; shameless cynicism and bragging; conceit — "woe unto them who are wise in their own eyes"; corrupt judges taking bribes; greedy and ignorant priests; immoral religion — that is, religion based on falsehoods. Isaiah spared no man, neither king nor prince, neither judge nor priest. But, somehow, by the grace of God, out of all this, a

[4] Isaiah 5.1-7

faithful few will emerge and they will bring a better world into being. "It shall come to pass at the end of days," is one of his favorite sentences.

Emanuel, God is With Us; the Prince of Peace.

One passage in the book of Isaiah has been a source of much debate, and — unfortunately — of deep resentment between Jews and Christians. The passage is what is known as the Emanuel passage in Isaiah 7.14–17.

It was the year 735 B.C.E. when, as we have already noted, the kings of Israel and Syria were pressing the King of Judah to join them in a war against Assyria. King Ahaz was confused, not knowing what to do. A deep crisis was hanging over the land. Young Isaiah was advising Ahaz not to allow himself to be dragged into war. He was urging that the "two tails of smoking firebrands," as he called the kings of Israel and Judah, would burn themselves out. Evidently a young woman with child was passing by. Isaiah pointed to her and said: by the time this woman has her child, and the child is old enough to reason, this crisis will have passed away. Young mothers will be naming their children after this great deliverance that was sure to come. For, Isaiah argued, "God is with us." The Hebrew word for it is "*Emanuel.*"

The early Christian church scholars interpreted this passage as referring to the birth of Jesus. Hence, they taught, Isaiah foretold the coming of Jesus.

Jewish scholars have rejected this interpretation. First, they have insisted the translation given in the Christian versions of the Bible passage is incorrect. Further, there are some seven hundred years between Isaiah and Jesus, and Isaiah was not the fortune telling kind of prophet who would foretell a birth seven hundred years later.[5]

Israel — The Servant of the Lord

Though he criticized his people sharply and mercilessly for their evil practices, Isaiah had a great and deep respect for what his people could and would do in history. Children of Abraham, Isaac and Jacob, following the teachings of Moses, liberated from Egypt and taken to "a land flowing with milk and honey," they were chosen by God to be His servant. From "the stock of Jesse," that is, from King David's descendants, a leader will arise, who shall be known as the Prince of Peace. He will bring justice and truth and peace into the world.

> And there shall come forth a shoot out
>   of the stock Jesse,
> And a twig shall grow forth out of his roots.
> And the spirit of the Lord shall rest upon him,
> The spirit of wisdom and understanding,
> The spirit of counsel and might,
> The spirit of knowledge and of the fear of the Lord.
> And his delight shall be in the fear of the Lord;
> And he shall not judge after the sight of his eyes,
> Neither decide after the hearing of his ears;
> But with righteousness shall he judge the poor,
> And decide with equity for the meek of the land;
> And he shall smite the land with the rod of his mouth,
> And with the breath of his lips shall he slay the wicked.

[5] The same debate carries over to the Servant of the Lord passages in Isaiah 9 and 11. Church scholars have pointed to these verses also, as foretelling the virgin birth of Jesus. This is a mistranslation of the Hebrew word *alma*, which means any young woman.

And righteousness shall be the girdle of his loins,
And faithfulness the girdle of his reins.
And the wolf shall dwell with the lamb,
And the leopard shall lie down with the kid;
And the calf and the young lion and the fatling together;
And a little child shall lead them.[6]

His people must be faithful to this vision of their duties in the world, and he was convinced that "a faithful remnant" there would always be to maintain this vision, however cruel and barbaric the world might be. In the later portions of the book of Isaiah, written by another man some two hundred or more years later, this idea is stressed even more. We shall study these later portions under the heading of The Second Isaiah.

It Shall Come to Pass

Isaiah is fond of saying, "It shall come to pass at the end of days." That expresses his optimism even in most difficult times. What he meant was that in time – in God's own good time – great and wonderful things will happen, if the people only do what is right. One of his most famous visions is the vision of universal peace:

And it shall come to pass in the end of days,
That the mountain of the Lord's house shall be established
At the head of the mountains,
And shall be exalted above the hills;
And all the nations shall stream unto it.

And many peoples shall go and say:
'Come ye, and let us go up to mountain of the Lord
To the house of the God of Jacob;

[6] Isaiah 11.1–6

That He may teach us of His ways
And that we may walk in His paths.'
For out of Zion shall go forth instruction,
And the word of the Lord from Jerusalem.

And He will judge between the nations,
And will arbitrate for many peoples;
And they will beat their swords into plowshares,
And their spears into pruning-hooks;
Nation shall not lift up sword against nation,
Neither shall they learn war any more.

O house of Jacob, come ye, and let us walk
In the light of the Lord.[7]

Religion must do its full share in bringing about the ideal world. In the opening chapter of the book of Isaiah, we have his definition of religion, which reminds us of Amos, Hosea, and Micah:

> Wash you, make you clean,
> Put away the evil of your doings
> From before Mine eyes,
> Cease to do evil;
> Learn to do well;
> Seek justice,
> Restrain the oppressor,
> Judge the fatherless,
> Plead for the widow.[8]

Despite the race hatreds, the nationalistic strife, the fanaticism of the bigots, the brutality of dictators, despite the intolerances and stupidities of men and nations, a better, juster world, lapped in law, "shall come to pass at the end of days." Isaiah lived by this faith and vision.

[7] Isaiah 2.2–5
[8] 1.16–17

TOPICS FOR FURTHER STUDY AND DISCUSSION

1. Draw a map and place the following in their proper places:
    a) The Tigris and Euphrates rivers; the Nile and the Jordan
       rivers; the Mediterranean Sea.
    b) Assyria, Egypt, Israel, Judah.
    What significance do you see in Judah's and Israel's geographic
    positions from the standpoint of wars?
2. Make a chronology of world events during the lifetime of
   Isaiah, that had to do with Judah and Israel.
3. To your "Who's Who" add the personalities who figure in this
   chapter.
4. Write a play or poem on Isaiah in the Temple when he heard
   the angel choir chanting *Holy, Holy, Holy* . . .
5. Were Isaiah living in your city, would he be speaking of the
   "wild grapes" of your city?   What would he point out as the
   "woes" of your city?
6. How many centuries were there between Isaiah and Jesus?
7. What did Isaiah mean by "The Servant of the Lord"?
   Who was the servant?
8. Who was the more optimistic: Amos, Hosea, Micah or Isaiah?
   Which one of these men would you want as your personal
   friend?

6. MICAH

It hath been told thee, O man, what is good,
And what the Lord doth require of thee:
Only to do justly, and to love mercy, and to walk humbly with
   thy God. (Micah 6.8)

ALL we know of the prophet Micah is his name and his country, Judah. We do not know the dates of his life. The best
that Bible scholars can do is to reason that he lived some fifty
years after Amos preached at Beth-El, or some thirty-five
years after Hosea. Isaiah was in his middle age when Micah
began his activity as prophet.

What manner of man was he? What sort of childhood or
youth did he have? Was he married? Did he have children?
What was his occupation? To all these questions we must
say: we don't know.

But we do know that he was one of the great prophets.
Like all of them, he was fearless in denouncing the evils of his
time. Judah was not as prosperous in his day as Israel had
been in the days of Amos. A good number of cities and towns
had grown up in the fifty years between Amos and Micah.
With these came many bad situations; crowding, unemployment, crime, as we noted in our chapter on Hosea. The
people and their governments had not yet learned how to care
for the unemployed, the widows and the orphans, the aged,
the sick. The rich were growing richer, and the poor were
growing poorer. The royalty, the military, the priests, the

politicians were self-seeking. Wars and threats of war, tribute to Assyria, were adding to the distress of the masses.

Micah reminds us of Amos in his attacks on the evils of his day; and he reminds us, also, of Hosea in his pleading for mercy and humility. Some scholars find in his words echoes of Isaiah. That is why they think that Micah was a young man when Isaiah was already well known as a prophet. Micah, they say, heard Isaiah speak, and was influenced by him. Some of Isaiah's phrases stuck in his mind.

Hear, I Pray You

Hear, I pray you, you heads of Jacob,
And rulers of the house of Israel:
Is it not for you to do justice,
You who hate the good and love the evil,
Who rob the skins from off them,
And their flesh from off their bones —
Who build Zion with blood,
And Jerusalem with iniquity?
The heads thereof judge for reward (i.e. bribes),
And the priests thereof teach for hire,
And the prophets thereof divine for money.[1]

The princes, the military people, the politicians, the priests, the false prophets — all were responsible for the evils in the land. Like all the prophets, Micah spoke angry words of protest, fearing no man.

He probably was an unpopular man. No one who criticizes the rich, the powerful, the popular heroes, is himself popular. The Hebrew prophets cared nothing for popularity, nor for money, nor for personal success. They had one supreme

[1] 3.1–2, 10

concern: to speak the truth as God gave them to see the truth.

Micah was especially critical of the city people. He is described by some scholars as "the prophet of the poor." These scholars think, therefore, that he was a peasant. He was convinced that the country was heading for collapse because of the lying, the cheating, the stealing he saw in the cities.

It Hath Been Told Thee, O Man

Micah is especially famous for one of the very great passages in the Bible. Every intelligent Jew and Christian should know this passage by heart. All through the two thousand six-seven hundred years since these words were first spoken by Micah, have they been quoted by Jews and non-Jews alike; for many, many centuries to come will people of all faiths continue to quote them:

Wherewith shall I come before the Lord,
And bow myself before God on high?
Shall I come before Him with burnt-offerings,
With calves of a year old?
Will the Lord be pleased with thousands of rams,
With ten thousands of rivers of oil?
Shall I give my first-born for my transgression,
The fruit of my body for the sin of my soul?
It hath been told thee, O man, what is good,
And what the Lord doth require of thee:
Only to do justly, and to love mercy, and to walk humbly with
thy God.[2]

Notice several points.

Wherewith shall I come . . . that is, how shall a man

[2] Micah 6.6–8

worship God? Micah is thinking of people going to the ancient Temple and what gifts they were to bring. *Bow myself before God* — that is, bowing in prayer.

Shall I come before him with burnt offerings . . . ? Micah is referring to animal sacrifices. Most people in ancient times offered animal sacrifices as an act of worship.

Shall I give my first-born for my transgression . . . ? The first-born son was offered as sacrifice to Moloch. Some Israelites took to this horrible practice. Moses and the prophets were violently against this. One of the great accomplishments of Moses, the prophets, and the later law-givers, is that they outlawed human sacrifice. Sternly the law of Moses commands:

Whoever he be of the children of Israel, or of the stranger that sojourn in Israel, that giveth of his seed (his children) unto Molech, he shall surely be put to death; the people of the land shall stone him with stones.[3]

You remember the story of Abraham and the sacrifice of Isaac, as told in Genesis 22. An unknown prophet wrote this story.

Father Abraham, the man who taught our biblical ancestors belief in the One God, was ready to obey God's command in all things, at all times, even to the point of sacrificing his beloved son Isaac; that was the test of his faith. But God Himself told the founder of our faith that He did not want human sacrifice. Animal sacrifice was good enough. Later the prophets condemned animal sacrifice too. Amos, you recall, argued, that what God wants of us is for every man to be just

[3] Lev. 20.2. *Molech* is another way of spelling *Moloch*. Read again chapter 2 of this book on idolatry.

to his fellow man. Hosea, soon after Amos, added that God wants every man to be merciful and loving to his fellow man. Micah added humility. Thus Micah accepted the teachings of both, Amos and Hosea, and added an important step to it. The later prophets and rabbis added still more, as we shall see: holiness, personal responsibility, prayer.

It hath been told thee, O man. Micah is speaking not alone to his fellow Israelites, but to all men: "It hath been told thee, O man . . ."; every man of every religion, of every race, of every nation. We speak of this as *universal,* as over against the *national,* the *racial,* or the *creedal.** The prophets loved their country, but they loved justice, mercy, humility, holiness even more. Beyond all was God.

TOPICS FOR FURTHER STUDY AND DISCUSSION

1. If Micah lived in your city today, which evil do you think would he attack most? Are there evils in your city? Explain.
2. Memorize Micah 6.6–8.
3. What is meant by *universal, national, creedal?* Does one preclude the other? Explain.
4. Is human sacrifice practiced today? Where?
5. Whose definition of religion do you like better, Isaiah's or Micah's. Try to improve on both.

* Look up these words in a large dictionary.

7. JEREMIAH

This is the covenant that I will make with the house of Israel after those days, saith the Lord: I will put my law in their inward parts, and in their hearts will I write it; and I will be their God and they will be my people.   (Jer. 31–33)

The Weeping Prophet

JEREMIAH was a sad and lonely man.   He has been called "the weeping prophet," "the man of sorrow."   One lone friend stood by him all his life; every one else scorned and ridiculed him.   His own family, including his mother, rejected him, he complains.   He was in and out of jail; he faced a military court, was sentenced to death and escaped by the skin of his teeth.   Several men took pity on him.   Once an Ethiopian slave saved him from a horrible death.   Highly sensitive, deeply religious, he was given to introspection.   Depressed by fears, he could also thrill with high hope.   His feelings shifted rapidly.   He gave expression to his moods and fears in haunting, musical words.   Probably illiterate, he, nevertheless, spoke some of the grandest poems in the Bible.   His constant talking and preaching made him unpopular, even hated; but he could not stop talking, much as he wanted to keep silent, he confesses.   The word of God burned in him, "like a flaming fire in my bones.   I weary myself to hold it in but can not." [1]

We know more of Jeremiah than we do of any other prophet.   Sensitive and gifted with great power of expression,

[1] 20.9

he talks about himself more than do the rest of the prophets. But the facts of his life are badly confused. In many instances it is impossible to tell which event he reports came first and which followed. That is because the book of Jeremiah is badly confused; many passages are misplaced.

The Story of a Book

Have you ever dropped your loose-leaf notebook, and the pages, unnumbered, spilled? Putting the pages back in the right order was difficult, and you must have misplaced some of them, however patiently you tried to put them back in proper sequence. If a friend, not familiar with your notes and compositions, tried to reassemble them for you, he would surely misplace some of the pages.

Jeremiah had been speaking and preaching for some twenty-two years to any one who would listen to him. But the crowds refused to listen; the King, the priests, the military persecuted him. They resented him and his predictions of disaster. One day, deeply discouraged, he dictated, from memory, to his friend Baruch, all he had been saying all those many years, hoping, as did Isaiah before him, that in time people would read his words and take them seriously. He dictated all his visions, poems, speeches. Scholars think that the reason he dictated all this material to Baruch, rather than write it down himself, is that he was illiterate.

This scroll was burned by the King in anger. We have an account of this in the book of Jeremiah.[2] We shall return to this chapter of his life a little later. Here we note how the book of Jeremiah came to be what it is in our hands.

[2] 36.22–23

Jeremiah, in anger, dictated his prophecies over again to Baruch, and added some more harsh words in the heat of anger. Later in his life he must have added more. This larger edition was copied again and again by later editors. The last copy was made, scholars think, about the year 200 B.C.E., several hundred years after the prophet's death. Some of these editors, no doubt, added a word or a phrase here and there; some wrote brief explanations in the margin of the skins or parchments; later editors embodied these marginal notes into the text itself. Some copyists made mistakes unknowingly. The result of all this is that the book of Jeremiah is a difficult one for scholars to rearrange back to the original dictations of the prophet. This is true, in part, of practically all the books of the Bible; it is especially true of the book of Jeremiah.

The Times of Jeremiah: The Fall of Assyria; the Rise of Babylon

The overwhelming fact in the lifetime of Jeremiah was the rise of a new world empire, Babylon. In the life of Isaiah, as we have noted, the world terror was Assyria. By the time of Jeremiah, Assyria was falling apart. Like blind Samson, the once mightiest empire on earth was staggering and collapsing. Conquered people were rebelling.

A new empire was arising, and that was Babylon, in the region of the Euphrates River. It was rich and powerful in every way. For a while the King of Egypt moved to help Assyria, Egypt's former enemy, out of fear of Babylon. But Egypt was weak and unreliable. On the way northeast to help Assyria, the Egyptian armies marched through Judah and slaughtered the King of Judah, the very good King Josiah. Jeremiah, like Isaiah before him, had urged the Judean king and army not to become involved with Egypt, for Egypt was like "a broken staff, which, if a man leans on it, collapses and pierces his hands."

The shadow of the plundering Babylonians hung over Judah, and kept Jeremiah frightened. In the end, in the year 586 B.C.E. we shall see a little later in our story, Babylon conquered Judah and the aged Jeremiah knew the most bitter sorrow in all his sad life.

The Reformation of Josiah

Another enormous thing happened in Judah during Jeremiah's lifetime. It is known in history as the *Reformation of Josiah*, or the *Deuteronomic Reformation*.

The book of Deuteronomy, the last of the five books of Moses, was produced during this time, and it created a revolution in the land. It made radical changes in the religious observances and in the economic life of the people. The local shrines devoted to the ba'alim, to Ashtoreth, to Moloch and to all the other idols were outlawed. Many priests were thrown out of work; all worship was concentrated in the Temple in Jerusalem; the laws of Moses, which had been badly ignored, were brought back; the ancient holidays, especially the Passover, were restored. All this meant distress in some parts of the country, and rejoicing among those who had opposed the idolatries practiced at these shrines. The purpose for bringing all worship into the Temple at Jerusalem, built by Solomon, was that it could be controlled better in one place.

In the book of Deuteronomy we have many reforms meant to improve the lot of the poor. It has been called "a prophetic law book," for the reason that it follows the teachings of the prophets in many instances. Some scholars think that Jeremiah had a hand in compiling this book; but this cannot be proved.[3]

Priestly Family — Villager

Jeremiah's life was tangled up in the life of his country. We cannot tell the story of his life apart from the history of Judah. And it was a stormy period — a time of revolution, foreign intrigues, invasion and, finally, the collapse of Judah and the deportation of many thousands of people to Babylon. We must report and read a double tragedy — the tragedy of a man bound up with the tragedy of his country. The events in the life of his country became events in his own life.

Jeremiah was born in a village on a hill some three miles northeast of Jerusalem. He must have looked long and often on the spires of the Holy City in the distance, and thought of the Temple and its worship. The exact year of his life we do not know, but it seems that he was born several years before 642 B.C.E. Some old people, when Jeremiah was a young boy, probably still remembered Isaiah.

He came of a family of priests, but there was no love between him and his priestly family. He complains that they were persecuting him. He never married. He was convinced, as were Amos, Hosea, Isaiah, that evil times were ahead, and he felt he had no right to bring children into such a distressful world.

[3] See the present author's *The Prophets: Their Personalities and Teachings* Chapter VIII.

In the year 625 B.C.E., when Jeremiah was about sixteen–seventeen years old, he had one of the worst scares of his life. The Scythians were on the march.

The Scythian Scare

The Scythians were a savage and cruel people; they had spilled over from the Caucasus Mountain area and invaded city after city along the Mediterranean Sea and were heading southward. Jeremiah was sure they were heading for Judah and Jerusalem. They were fierce barbarians, huge of build (the Greeks liked to employ them as policemen). He thought that they were punishment God was sending upon Judah for the many evils in the land. In his excited imagination he saw Jerusalem in ruins and the whole land laid waste. One of his most vivid poems comes from this fear that had gripped him:

> Behold, he cometh up as clouds,
> And his chariots are as the whirlwind;
> His horses are swifter than eagles.
> Woe unto us! for we are undone.[4]

A picture of a land in ruins, as if hit by an atomic bomb, flashes before him:

> I beheld the earth,
> And, lo, it was waste and void;
> And the heavens, and they had no light.
> I beheld the mountains, and, lo, they trembled,
> And all the hills moved to and fro.
> I beheld, and, lo, there was no man.
> And all the birds of the heavens were fled.

[4] 4.13

> I beheld, and, lo, the fruitful field was a wilderness,
> And all the cities thereof were broken down
> At the presence of the Lord,
> And before His fierce anger.[5]

The Scythians changed their course; Judah escaped. Many must have said that Jeremiah was a panicky prophet.

Inaugural Vision

Like Isaiah before him — and like Moses about seven hundred years earlier — Jeremiah hesitated and was afraid to accept his duties as prophet. He describes his feelings in what is now Chapter 1 of his book. He fights off the voice within him; he pleads that he is too young, too inexperienced, too weak. "Ah, Lord God, I cannot speak, for I am only a child." But the voice persists and haunts him, and finally overwhelms him. Speak he must, and he must speak the truth, as God speaks it to him in his solitude, in his loneliness. He must fear no man — neither king, nor prince, nor priest, nor the crowds. And speak he did, fearlessly, passionately, for about forty years.

The Young Prophet Speaks

Like all the prophets, Jeremiah spared no man. He attacked evil wherever he saw it. King, priest, prophet, judge, politician — all were guilty of taking advantage of the poor, all were concerned only with their personal gain:

> From the prophet even unto the priest
> Every one dealeth falsely.[6]

[5] 4.23–26
[6] 8.1C

Like all the prophets, he condemned idolatry in angry, bitter words:

For the children of Judah have done that which is evil in My sight, saith the Lord; they have set their detestable things in the house whereon My name is called, to defile it. And they have built the high places of Topheth, which is in the valley of the son of Hinnom, to burn their sons and their daughters in the fire; (something) which I commanded not, neither came it into My mind.[7]

From the name Hinnom is derived the Hebrew *Gei-Hinnom,* which corresponds to the Christian word *Hell* — the place for all that is evil, the most frightful place imaginable. In present day Israel tourists are led to a spot from which they may view this desolate place, made so notorious by the fact that in this ravine were dumped the bones of children sacrificed to Moloch.

Prophet of Disaster

Jeremiah was convinced that evil days were ahead and expressed his belief in powerful terms. Once he took a clay bottle, secured a number of men to follow him to the horrible valley of Hinnom. Curious onlookers probably followed. There he enacted a little drama. He unburdened himself of an angry speech, denouncing the king, the military, the priests and the people for their idolatries, and flung the vessel on the rocky soil, smashing it into fragments.

Even so will I break this people and this city, as one breaketh a potter's vessel, that can not be made whole again.[8]

[7] 7.30–31
[8] 19.11

Temple Sermon and Trial

One sermon Jeremiah preached many times. It is usually referred to as the Temple Sermon. He delivered it from the steps of the Temple to a large and curious crowd. It reminds us of Amos at Beth-El.

A huge crowd was milling about in front of the Temple, crowding the one hundred fifty steps leading to its entrance. Jeremiah took his place as best he could and delivered an angry sermon. He warned the people that the alliance with Egypt against Babylon would end in catastrophe. The military people and the priests were feeding them lies. Their buildings would not stand up before the enemy. Their Temple would not save them. There is no security in fortifications and temples. We see him on the steps speaking to an astonished crowd:

Hear the word of the Lord, all ye of Judah, that enter in at these gates to worship the Lord. Thus saith the Lord of hosts, the God of Israel: Amend your ways and your doings, and I will cause you to dwell in this place. Trust ye not in lying words, saying: 'The temple of the Lord, the temple of the Lord, the temple of the Lord, are these.' Nay, but if ye thoroughly amend your ways and your doings; if ye thoroughly execute justice between a man and his neighbour; if ye oppress not the stranger, the fatherless, and the widow, and shed not innocent blood in this place, neither walk after other gods to your hurt; then will I cause you to dwell in this place, in the land that I gave to your fathers, for ever and ever. Behold, ye trust in lying words, that cannot profit. Will ye steal, murder, and commit adultery, and swear falsely, and offer unto Baal, and walk after other gods whom ye have not known, and come and stand before Me in this house, whereupon My name is called and say: 'We are delivered,' that ye may do all these abominations? Is this house, whereupon My name is called, become a den of robbers in your eyes? [9]

A country is safe only when it is just in all its dealings. He warned against "lying words" and false hopes.

He was promptly arrested and charged with treason. We have a report of this in chapter 26 of the book of Jeremiah:

Now it came to pass, when Jeremiah had an end of speaking all that the Lord had commanded him to speak unto all the people, that the priests and the prophets and all the people laid hold on him, saying: 'Thou shalt surely die. Why hast thou prophesied in the name of the Lord, saying: This house shall be like Shiloh, and this city shall be desolate, without an inhabitant?' And all the people were gathered against Jeremiah in the house of the Lord.

When the princes of Judah heard these things, they came up from the king's house unto the house of the Lord; and they sat in the entry of the new gate of the Lord's house. Then spoke the priests and the prophets unto the princes and to all the people, saying: 'This man is worthy of death; for he hath prophesied against this city, as ye have heard with your ears.'

Jeremiah's conduct before this military court is one of the bravest scenes in history. Calmly, quietly he admits that he had said all he is charged with saying; he even makes it more emphatic. He does not try to back down, does not attempt to explain away his words; he does not seek to excuse himself for his speech. He does not ask for mercy. He is neither humble nor defiant. His personal safety does not worry him. All that concerns him is that he speaks God's word faithfully.

[9] 7.2–11

Then spoke Jeremiah unto all the princes and to the people, saying: 'The Lord sent me to prophesy against this house and against
this city all the words that ye have heard. Therefore now amend
your ways and your doings, and hearken to the voice of the Lord
your God; and the Lord will repent Him of the evil that He
hath pronounced against you. But as for me, behold, I am in
your hand; do with me as is good and right in your eyes. Only
know ye for certain that, if ye put me to death, ye will bring innocent blood upon yourselves, and upon this city, and upon the
inhabitants thereof; for of a truth the Lord hath sent me unto you
to speak all these words in your ears.' [10]

A tumult followed. Some argued that Jeremiah had the
right to speak as he did. Others had done it. Some argued
that he was guilty of treason and should be put to death. He
was declared guilty; but, fortunately, several influential men
took pity on him and spirited him away.

Jeremiah Writes Down His Prophecies

Following this experience, broken-hearted that no one listened to him, convinced that the country was plunging into
disaster, he decided to write down all that was on his heart
and mind. He dictated all he had been saying to his faithful
friend, Baruch, and asked him to go to the Temple and there
read it in the hearing of the people. Baruch did that. The
people listened in astonishment. Baruch was promptly arrested and interrogated; the police, however, were decent to
him and allowed him to escape.

And they said unto him: "Sit down now, and read it in our
ears." So Baruch read it in their ears. Now it came to pass,

[10] 26.8–15
Does this trial remind you of any other famous trial in history?

when they had heard all the words, they turned in fear one toward another, and said unto Baruch: "We will surely tell the king
of all these words." And they asked Baruch, saying: "Tell us
now: How didst thou write all these words at his mouth?" Then
Baruch answered them: "He pronounced all these words unto me
with his mouth, and I wrote them with ink in the book." Then
said the princes unto Baruch: "Go, hide thee, thou and Jeremiah;
and let no man know where ye are." And they went in to the
king into the court; but they had deposited the roll in the cham-
ber of Elishama the scribe; and they told all the words in the ears
of the king.[11]

A report of this reached the King, Jehoiakim, who hated
Jeremiah. He ordered the scroll read to him. We have a
description of the scene:

Now the king was sitting in the winter-house in the ninth
month; and the brazier was burning before him. And it came to
pass, when Jehudi had read three or four columns, that he cut it
with the penknife, and cast it into the fire that was in the brazier,
until all the roll was consumed in the fire that was in the brazier.[12]

Thus was Jeremiah's book burned. The prophet, however,
very fortunately, escaped. When word reached him that his
prophecies had been burned, in a fit of anger he dictated them
anew to his friend Baruch, and added much more to it. This,
in time, became the book of Jeremiah as we have it.[13]

The Country Invaded

Jeremiah's worst fears came true. In the year 597 B.C.E.
the Babylonians, under the leadership of Nebuchadnezzar, in-

---

[11] 36.15–20
[12] 36.22–23
[13] See pages 51–52 in this book.

vaded Jerusalem and the Temple, plundered and burned without mercy, carried off into exile some ten thousand men, women and children, especially the young and the skilled, took the King and his court and the military leaders as prisoners.

Left behind were the old, the sick, the crippled, the helpless. Nebuchadnezzar appointed a puppet as governor. His duties were to keep the Israelites from rebelling and to extract as much in taxes as possible.

What Jeremiah had foretold came true. He was brokenhearted. In his own heart he was hoping against hope. What was he doing and saying at this time?

He had advised coming to terms with Nebuchadnezzar not because he liked the Babylonian invader, but because he was convinced it was nothing but suicide to oppose him. By coming to terms with him, something of Judah might be saved; certainly lives would be saved.

To make his point he seems to have walked about in the streets of Jerusalem with twisted bars around his neck, in the form of a yoke. Again we see a prophet act in a highly unusual manner. Isaiah, we recall, had walked through the streets of Jerusalem almost naked. Jeremiah was trying to say to the people: Resistance to the Babylonians would lead only to the yoke of slavery, imposed by this cruel conqueror.

Once at least, that we know of, he was attacked and beaten for this conduct.

Jeremiah Writes a Letter

To the refugees in Babylon Jeremiah wrote a letter, which has become famous in Jewish history. The advice he gives his people in this letter is the policy Jews have followed all through their history, in the many lands in which they have lived, to our own time:

Build ye houses and dwell in them, and plant gardens, and eat the fruit in them; take ye wives, and beget sons and daughters; and take wives for your sons, and give your daughters to husbands, that they may bear sons and daughters; and multiply ye there, and be not diminished. And seek the peace of the city whither I have caused you to be carried away captive, and pray unto the Lord for it; for in the peace thereof shall ye have peace.[14]

What Jeremiah was telling his people was: Live normally, adjust yourselves to your new environment, but be faithful to your religion at the same time. He urged what we today call "integration," and "religious liberty." Nationally, Jews are good citizens of the countries in which they live; religiously, they are faithful Jews.

586 B.C.E. — *Exile*

There was talk of resistance to Babylon. A new Pharaoh came to the throne of Egypt. He was making a great noise of rebelling against the Babylonians and throwing out the invaders. A new king came to the throne of Judah, a weak man by the name of Zedekiah. He was inclined to join the Egyptians. The Judean patriots, more zealous than wise, were urging him to do that. Jeremiah was against it, and, as always, spoke his mind in bold words. He was convinced that only total destruction of Judah would result.

Jeremiah was scorned. The people did not understand him.

[14] 29.5–7

They thought he was a traitor. One day he was attacked and thrown into a cesspool. By sheer good fortune, he was saved. We have an account of this:

> So Ebed-melech took the men with him, and went into the house of the king under the treasury, and took thence worn clouts and worn rags, and let them down by cords into the pit to Jeremiah. And Ebed-melech the Ethiopian said unto Jeremiah: "Put now these worn clouts and rags under thine armholes under the cords." And Jeremiah did so. So they drew up Jeremiah with the cords, and took him up out of the pit; and Jeremiah remained in the court of the guard.[15]

Zedekiah yielded to the clamor of the zealous patriots and rebelled against Nebuchadnezzar. The Babylonian army struck back swiftly and ruthlessly, and besieged the city. Siege meant famine, disease, death for men, women and children, the young and the aged alike. This siege lasted for a year and a half.

Jeremiah Buys a Parcel of Land

But even in this black hour Jeremiah, who had been predicting the worst, still had faith that a time would come when Judah would be rebuilt and the people restored to their own. He expressed this in a dramatic manner, as always.

One day a cousin came to him and said that there was a parcel of land owned by his family, on which Jeremiah had the first claim, according to the laws of Moses. Jeremiah bought this land as a symbol to the people. Though he had prophesied destruction, over and over again, he believed ultimately the people would be restored to their own land; he was

[15] 38.11–13

willing to invest in the land now under the heels of the invader. We have a good description of this purchase and act of faith:

> Thus saith the Lord of hosts, the God of Israel: Take these deeds; this deed of purchase, both that which is sealed, and this deed which is open, and put them in an earthen vessel; that they may continue many days. For thus saith the Lord of hosts, the God of Israel: Houses and fields and vineyards shall yet again be bought in this land.[16]

Ninth Day of Ab, 586

In the summer of 586 B.C.E. — on the ninth day of the month of Ab, which has become the saddest day in Jewish history, and kept as a fast by the faithful — the gates of Jerusalem finally fell to the Babylonian army, the enemy poured into the city and the Temple, reduced everything to the ground, burning, killing without pity. King Zedekiah watched his own children slaughtered. They pulled his own eyes out of their sockets, and led him away in chains to Babylon, a prisoner of war. No laws protected prisoners of war in those days.

Jeremiah was offered special favor by the Babylonians. Had he not urged his people to surrender to them? They thought he was their friend. They did not understand him. He scorned their offer and chose to remain with his own. They did not know what was in Jeremiah's heart. And they did not know that he had spoken fiercely against them and prophesied their doom. The just judgments of God would fall upon the barbarians.

[16] 32.14–15

Thus Shall Babylon Sink

In his own mind, Babylon would go up in smoke even as she had burned and pillaged Jerusalem and Judah. To one who was leaving on the long march to Babylon as a refugee he gave a parchment, on which he had written these words and more:

> Though Babylon should mount up to heaven,
> And though she should fortify the heights of her strength,
> Yet from me shall spoilers come unto her, saith the Lord . . .
> For the spoiler is come upon her, even upon Babylon,
> And her mighty men are taken,
> Their bows are shattered;
> For the Lord is a God of recompense,
> He will surely requite.[17]

He asked this refugee to read all this to the people, as his encouragement to them, and then tie this parchment to a stone and fling it into the Euphrates, as a symbol that Babylonia would sink to the bottom of deep waters and never come up.

Thus shall Babylon sink, and shall not rise, because the evil that I am bringing upon her.[18]

Just what finally happened to Jeremiah we can not tell with certainty. He was probably swept along with the crowds fleeing to Egypt for refuge — the Egypt he had scorned all his life. There he went to his unknown grave, ridiculed by his fellow refugees as a false prophet. In history he towers as one of the greatest prophets we have had.

[17] 51.53–56
[18] 51.64

The New Covenant

One great hope sustained Jeremiah all his life. He believed, no matter how terrible life was, that a God of justice and compassion would save His people. What mattered it if the Temple were in rubble and Jerusalem in ruins? God's covenant with Israel was eternal. God is everlastingly true, just and merciful. This covenant between God and Israel was not in the Temple, not in sacrifices, not in any building or organization, or ritual. It was in the heart of every man. Israel would surely arise from her calamities a better, juster, nobler people. Israel will be a faithful people, even as Amos, Hosea, Micah, and Isaiah had taught.

This is the covenant that I will make with the house of Israel after those days, saith the Lord; I will put my law in their inward parts, and in their hearts will I write it; and I will be their God and they shall be my people . . . for I will forgive their iniquity and their sins will I remember no more.[19]

Despite his foretelling calamity all his life, despite his living through one disaster after another, Jeremiah was a man of faith. Ultimately, in God's own time, a happier day will come, and Israel shall rejoice and sing. For the hand of God it was that was shaping history and determining all things.

The Potter and the Clay

One day he found himself watching a potter working at his wheel, shaping a vessel. He was fascinated. The potter put a lump of clay to the wheel and shaped it into form. Then he held up his work and examined it critically; he did not like it.

[19] 31.33–34

It was out of line. It was lopsided. He must make a perfect vessel. Jeremiah watched this man crush the vessel and put it to the wheel anew. He must have a perfect form, lovely and graceful.

As Jeremiah watched this man at work, a thought flashed through his mind: that is the way God deals with mankind. All these wars, and burnings and killings, the rise and fall of nations, were God's mysterious ways of applying pressure on mankind in the shaping of a perfect humanity.

Then the word of the Lord came to me, saying: "O house of Israel, cannot I do with you as this potter? saith the Lord. Behold, as the clay in the potter's hand, so are ye in My hand, O house of Israel. At one instant I may speak concerning a nation, and concerning a kingdom, to pluck up and to break down and to destroy it; but if that nation turn from their evil, because of which I have spoken against it, I repent of the evil that I thought to do unto it . . ." [20]

That was his undying faith, and he gave expression to it in musical lines, more than once.

From afar the Lord appeared unto me.
'Yea, I have loved thee with an everlasting love;
Therefore with affection have I drawn thee.
Again I will build, and thou shalt be built,
O virgin of Israel;
Again shalt thou be adorned with thy tabrets,
And shalt go forth in the dances of them that make merry.
Again shalt thou plant vineyards upon the mountains of Samaria;
The planters shall plant, and shall have the use thereof.
For there shall be a day,

[20] 18.5–8

That the watchmen shall call upon the mount Ephraim:
Arise ye, and let us go up to Zion,
Unto the Lord our God.'

For thus saith the Lord:
Sing with gladness for Jacob,
And shout at the head of the nations;
Announce ye, praise ye, and say:
'O Lord, save Thy people,
The remnant of Israel.' [21]

TOPICS FOR FURTHER STUDY AND DISCUSSION

1. On your map in connection with Isaiah, showing Judah, Israel, Egypt and Assyria, add Babylon. Of what significance is that?
2. To your Chronology, add the basic facts in the history of the time of Jeremiah. Of what significance are these facts in the history of Judah and the life of Jeremiah? See any good Bible history book, such as Harry M. Orlinsky, *Ancient Israel;* Ira M. Price, *The Dramatic Story of the Old Testament;* Bernhard W. Anderson, *Understanding the Old Testament.* See, also, the present author's, *The Prophets: Their Personalities and Teachings,* Chapter VIII.
3. How many years are there between Jeremiah and Isaiah? Between Jeremiah and Amos? Hosea?
4. Compare the inaugural vision of Isaiah (Is. 6) with the inaugural vision of Jeremiah (Jer. 1). Which of the two do you prefer? Why?
5. *Ah, Lord God, I can not speak.* Compare this with
   a) Isaiah (6.8), *Here am I, send me;* b) with Abraham (Gen. 22.1), *Here am I;* c) Moses (Exod. 3.11 ff). Why was one man reluctant to heed the call while another readily accepted?
6. Jeremiah criticized his king and the military leaders in time of war, and urged surrender or collaboration with the enemy. Was he, therefore, a traitor? Do we consider a man a traitor

[21] 31.3–7

or a patriot who speaks that way in time of war?   Explain your position.

7. Write a play or a dialogue on any one of the following:
   a) Jeremiah on the steps of the Temple delivering his Temple Sermon;
   b) Jeremiah before the military court;
   c) King Jehoiakim burning Baruch's scroll.
   d) Jeremiah and a Babylonian officer who is offering him asylum in Babylon.

8. Who in your judgment was the greater prophet, Isaiah or Jeremiah?   Explain.

9. How wise is it for Jews today to follow the advice Jeremiah gave in his letter to the refugees in Babylon?   Explain.

8. BY THE WATERS OF BABYLON

A LONG, long line of men and women — thousands upon thousands of them, as far as the eye could see — bundles on their backs, children in their arms, some small animals, perhaps, trailing by their sides, was moving slowly under a hot sun. They were Judean refugees, dragging themselves northeastward into exile, under the whip of their Babylonian invaders. They were a sad and tragic lot, as are all people who are torn from home and country and forced by an invading army into a foreign land.

All they had loved had gone up in smoke: their country, their Holy City, their Temple, their homes. Their families were torn apart; parents and grandparents, too old to work for the invaders, the sick, the crippled, were abandoned, with none to care for them. Some had fled to Egypt for refuge. Only the young, the strong and the skilled were taken into Babylon. They were to help build a new and mighty empire for the invaders.

Their king, Zedekiah, blinded and in chains, was dragging along with them; his sons had been slain before his own eyes. The royal court was murdered. The priests and the sweet singers of their psalms in the sanctuary built by King Solomon were done to death or were forced to join the refugees as prisoners of war. This happened in the summer of the year 586 B.C.E., the final deportation of the Judeans into Babylonian exile.

All that Jeremiah — and the prophets before him — had

foretold came true. Some must have recalled the warnings spoken by Isaiah, Micah, Hosea and Amos — as rehearsed by their parents and grandparents — and felt guilty. They had not heeded the warnings of these men of God and thus brought the tragedy of exile on their own heads. They had sinned; bitter memories haunted them. And they were fearful. God Himself, they were convinced, had abandoned them. Their sins had overtaken them.

A Babylonian soldier taunted them: Why are you so depressed, you Judeans, once so happy in your own Jerusalem? Where is your Almighty God? Why is He not protecting you? Why so fearful? Why so glum? "Come, sing us one of the songs of Zion."

One of the refugees, a gifted poet, wrote a poem giving expression to the sadness in the hearts of all of them, and also to their defiant pledge of loyalty to Jerusalem and the Temple. This poem has come down to us as Psalm 137:

> By the waters of Babylon,
> There we sat down, yea, we wept,
> When we remembered Zion.
> Upon the willows in the midst thereof
> We hanged up our harps.
> For there they that led us captive asked of us words of song,
> And our tormentors asked of us mirth:
> 'Sing us one of the songs of Zion.'
> How shall we sing the Lord's song
> In a foreign land?
>
> If I forget thee, O Jerusalem,
> Let my right hand forget her cunning.
> Let my tongue cleave to the roof of my mouth,

If I remember thee not;
If I set not Jerusalem
Above my chiefest joy.

Nebuchadnezzar was a shrewd empire builder. He settled these Judean refugees in one of the richest parts of his country, where the soil was good and water was plentiful, and gave them all the freedom they wanted to organize their own lives as they saw fit, including the freedom to worship as they pleased. By this method he sought to win their loyalty and cooperation. They prospered as farmers, or in commerce. Their children quickly learned the language and the ways of the Babylonians, and were soon forgetting their Judean traditions, including their religion. The faithful men and women, who wanted to remain true to their religion, were deeply distressed. How might they remain true to their faith? How might they train their children to remain faithful? "How shall we sing the Lord's song in a foreign land?"

They were free to build a new Temple. The Babylonians permitted them to do it; but the laws of Moses prohibited it. Only in Jerusalem might the Temple of God stand, and Jerusalem was now far, far away, settled by a mixed people who neglected it badly. Where once the Temple of Solomon had stood in all its glory, there wild beasts prowled for prey.

The people needed comforting, feeling guilty and fearful as they did. They needed guidance and encouragement. Someone had to convince them that God had not abandoned them, that He was with them, though they were far away from Jerusalem and the Temple; someone had to give them hope for a new life. Several prophets and poets spoke the badly needed words of consolation. The only one of these

whom we know by name, and in whose name a book has
come down to us, is Ezekiel.

TOPICS FOR FURTHER STUDY AND DISCUSSION

1. On your map, trace the route of the Judean exiles on the way
   to Babylon. Show where in Babylon they settled. (See any
   good history book; the titles already suggested are very good.)
2. On your Chronology indicate the dates of the Babylonian Exile, the first and second deportations, and the date when the
   Babylonian exiles began returning to Jerusalem.
3. On your "Who's Who" table, add the names of those who figure prominently in the history of the Babylonian Exile.
4. Write a dialogue between the Babylonian soldier and the Judean exiles as background for Psalm 137.
5. Find a musical recording of Psalm 137 and play it in class.
6. What were the problems the refugees in Babylon had to solve
   to normalize their lives?
   What advice had they received from Jeremiah?

9. EZEKIEL

And He said unto me, Son of Man, stand upon thy feet, and I will speak unto thee. (Ezekiel 2.1)

EZEKIEL is known as the "prophet of reconstruction." He lived with the exiles in Babylon when the religious life of the Judeans had to be reconstructed in every detail. He encouraged, guided and urged his people to rebuild their shattered life as a religious community, and gave them the basic principles to guide them in this reconstruction. For this reason he is considered by many scholars as one of the most influential persons in the entire history of Judaism.

Ezekiel spoke of himself as "a watchman over the house of Israel."

So thou, son of man, I have set thee a watchman over the house of Israel; therefore, when thou shalt hear the word at My mouth, warn them from Me.[1]

He spoke of himself, also, as the shepherd of his people. Observing his fellow Judeans in exile, scattered as they were, far from their native land and beloved Jerusalem, he thought of them as scattered sheep needing a shepherd to guide and protect them.

My sheep wandered through all the mountains, and upon every high hill; yea, upon all the face of the earth were my sheep scattered, and there was none that did search or seek.[2]

[1] 33.7
[2] 34.4

A faithful, alert shepherd he was, constantly on the lookout for signs of danger, bravely sounding the alarm when he felt that danger threatened. He condemned the many false prophets — or false "shepherds," as he referred to them — who spoke only what people wanted to hear, thus winning favor for themselves and gaining popularity. The faithful shepherd must be concerned with the well-being of his flock, not his personal advantage.

Biography

Ezekiel was born into a priestly family. He considered himself a descendant of Zadok, who was a descendant of Aaron, brother of Moses, and the founder of the priestly class. He spoke and thought and taught more like a priest than did any other of the prophets. He was fond of the ritual of the priests, its pomp and pageantry, concerned himself with the laws of the priests, and all his life dreamed and spoke of the time when the Temple would be restored and the priests would return to their duties, once again officiating at the sacrifices. The other prophets looked disdainfully upon this ritual.

In the year 597 B.C.E. Ezekiel was carried off into Babylon. He was probably in his teens then. Jeremiah was an old man at this time, very much of a storm center. Did Ezekiel hear him speak? We do not know. He settled in Tel-Abib, a village in a rich, fertile valley. There, for twenty-two years, he served as "shepherd" of the confused and unhappy people, cheering and comforting them. His house seems to have been a meeting place of the leaders of the community; we read of gatherings in his home. There are references to his wife. He seems to have had a sweet voice; people loved to hear him speak. And he complains about this: people like to hear him, but do not do as he asks them to do.

. . . lo, thou art unto them as a love song of one that hath a pleasant voice, and can play well on an instrument; so they hear thy words but do them not.[3]

Ezekiel was the strangest of all the prophets. He spoke in fantastic terms. Highly imaginative, often agitated, he spoke in extravagant, sometimes wild, images. The reader of his book cannot always tell whether what he is reading is fact or fiction, an actual report or imagination. He repeats himself over and over again. He is fond of certain phrases and is always using them. One of his pet phrases, "son of man," occurs in his book about a hundred times. Yet his book is the most orderly and neatly arranged of any of the prophetic books. Unlike Jeremiah, he wrote his own book and carefully edited it.

Images

Ezekiel's imagery is gorgeous and brilliant, but highly baffling. We are left confused, even bewildered. He explains his visions in detail, and the more he explains the more bewildering some of them become.

We recall only a few of his visions and images.

His inaugural vision is most fantastic, unlike the inaugural visions of any of the other prophets we have read. The closest to it is Isaiah's vision as reported in chapter 6 of the book of Isaiah, which we have already studied.

In the first chapter of his book, Ezekiel gives us a dazzling picture.*

[3] 33.32
* The teacher and class might read Ezekiel 1.

A furious storm tears the heavens into shreds. Lightning flashes; a great cloud, with glowing embers in its lap, is swaying over his head. The earth trembles. From the ominous, menacing sky, emerge fiery chariots, wheels within wheels; he sees the throne of God. He sees flaming torches in the heavens. Four peculiar creatures appear in the depths above him — creatures no man had ever seen or imagined. Each has four faces — of a man, a lion, an ox and an eagle. Each has four wings. These creatures move in straight lines, never making a curve, or cutting an angle. He sees brilliant jewels, glistening in the black clouds, like live coals; he hears the rustle of wings. He reports: "And when they moved, I heard the noise of their wings, like the noise of great waters, like the voice of the Almighty . . ." A throne of glowing sapphire emerges in faint outline. The young prophet is overwhelmed and falls to the ground. He hears a voice, "Son of man, stand upon thy feet, and I will speak unto thee."

What did he mean to tell us by means of this imagery? In detail it is impossible to tell, and we should not try to give a specific meaning to each detail. That is the way great poets of all people express themselves, as for instance, Coleridge in his *Ancient Mariner*, or Dante in his *Inferno*. Basically, he is saying what all the other prophets said in their inaugural visions: the awesome presence of God rests upon him; he feels himself called and dedicated as prophet; he hears and obeys the voice of God, which is an overwhelming power in his life: "Thus saith the Lord." Like all the other prophets, what Ezekiel is saying is that he must stand on his own feet, bravely, courageously, hear the Word and speak as the messenger of the Lord.

He is not always that confused and confusing. Some of his

images are clear. We may cite several examples. He compares Judah to a young lioness, rearing her whelps into frisky, tearing young lions; he speaks of Judah, also, as a clinging vine bursting with sap and life by water courses. Egypt he compares to a crocodile that is fouling her waters. Nebuchadnezzar, the Babylonian who had plundered the world and destroyed Judah and Jerusalem, is a giant speckled eagle, with enormous wings, a swooping menace.

Prophet of Reconstruction

It was not only Jerusalem and the Temple that lay in ruins; the hearts of the people were deeply distressed, and their minds were confused. Their spirits were depressed. Many felt bitter and cynical. The good and the bad alike were crushed by the disaster that had befallen them; the innocent and the guilty were being punished indiscriminately. If God is just, why does He permit this? Why must the innocent suffer along with the guilty? And why were they more guilty than their fathers were? It was their fathers who had sinned; punishment, however, fell upon their children. Why? "Our transgressions and our sins are upon us, and we pine away in them; how then shall we live?" [4]

Ezekiel urged two principles to guide the people's thinking: 1) the freedom and the responsibility of every man; 2) repentance. These became established principles in Judaism to the present day.

[4] 33.10

1. Freedom and Personal Responsibility

People were saying in Ezekiel's time: "The fathers have eaten sour grapes and the children's teeth are set on edge." Why? God must be unjust if He permits the children to suffer for the sins of the fathers.

Ezekiel denies this.

> The word of the Lord came unto me, saying: What mean ye that ye use this proverb in the land of Israel, saying:
>> The fathers have eaten sour grapes,
>> And the children's teeth are set on edge?
> As I live, saith the Lord God, ye shall not have occasion any more to use this proverb in Israel. Behold, all souls are Mine; as the soul, of the father, so also the soul of the son is Mine; the soul that sinneth, it shall die.[5]

That is, every man shall suffer for his own sins. Ezekiel argues this with much emphasis. If a man is righteous he is rewarded for his virtue; if he is wicked, he is punished for his wickedness. One will not suffer for the sins of the other. Every man is free to be righteous or wicked; if he is righteous he is rewarded; if he is wicked he is punished.

2. Repentance

Further — and this is basic in the teachings of Ezekiel — a wicked man need not perish. He can repent, sincerely and devoutly, and save himself from God's punishment. To this day Ezekiel's teaching on this score is emphasized in Judaism, especially on the Day of Atonement, when one of Ezekiel's great passages is read in synagogues:

[5] 18.1–4

Cast away from you all your transgressions, wherein ye have transgressed; and make you a new heart and a new spirit; for why will ye die, O house of Israel? For I have no pleasure in the death of him that dieth, saith the Lord God; wherefore turn yourselves, and live.[6] *

In the Valley of Dry Bones

Ezekiel was anxious, at all times, to build up hope in his people. Their exile will come to an end, he assured them; their Temple will be rebuilt. They will return to Zion renewed and reborn as God's people. He gave expression to this in one of his most famous visions.

The hand of God rests upon him, he feels. He is transported to a mountain, whence he sees a valley filled with the skeletons and bones of men, bleaching in the sun.

And He caused me to pass by them round about, and, behold, there were very many in the open valley; and lo, they were very dry. And He said unto me: "Son of man, can these bones live?" And I answered: "O Lord God, Thou knowest." Then He said unto me: "Prophesy over these bones, and say unto them: O ye dry bones, hear the word of the Lord: Thus saith the Lord God unto these bones: Behold, I will cause breath to enter into you, and ye shall live. And I will lay sinews upon you, and will bring up flesh upon you, and cover you with skin, and put breath in you, and ye shall live; and ye shall know that I am the Lord." So I prophesied as I was commanded; and as I prophesied, there was a noise, and behold a commotion, and the bones came together, bone to its bone. And I beheld, and, lo, there were sinews upon them,

---

[6] 18.31–32

* Do you agree with Ezekiel that one generation does not suffer for the sins of the preceding generation? Do you agree with him, further, that every person is free and able to change his ways? What kind of world would we have if we did not insist that every person is free and able to change his ways and be personally responsible for his own conduct?

and flesh came up, and skin covered them above; but there was no breath in them. Then said He unto me: "Prophesy unto the breath, prophesy, son of man, and say to the breath: Thus saith the Lord God: Come from the four winds, O breath, and breathe upon these slain, that they may live." So I prophesied as He commanded me, and the breath came into them, and they lived, and stood up upon their feet, an exceeding great host.[7]

A New Heart Will I Give You

Meantime, Ezekiel urged faith and unity. Again he resorts to a symbolic act: he takes two sticks, writes on one, "For Judah," and on the other, "For Ephraim," * and ties the two sticks together. The divided nation shall be bound into one — one and indivisible. God will gather His scattered flock and bring them back to His holy mountain.

Ezekiel lived by faith and taught his people faith. To encourage them in their faith he described for them the restored Temple and its services. He is carried by a spirit to Jerusalem, and describes in precise detail all he has seen in the new Temple. Scholars marvel at the detailed description he gives. This flight, carried by his hair, he reports as a fact.

Over and over he urged faith on his distressed people, and repentance. One of the most famous passages is repeated in synagogues on the Day of Atonement, as a basic teaching of Judaism:

A new heart also will I give you, and a new spirit will I put within you; and I will take away the stony heart out of your flesh,

---

[7] 37.2–10
Do you know any other famous poem where an angel guides one to see and observe most unusual sights?
* Another name for northern Israel, since Ephraim was the largest of the ten tribes.

and I will give you a heart of flesh. And I will put my spirit within you, and cause you to walk in My statutes, and ye shall keep Mine ordinances, and do them. And ye shall dwell in the land that I gave to your fathers; and ye shall be My people, and I will be your God.[8]

TOPICS FOR FURTHER STUDY AND DISCUSSION

1. What is meant by "a period of reconstruction?" Have you read of such periods in any history you have studied?
2. On your map indicate the area where Nebuchadnezzar settled the Judean exiles.
3. If a publisher, planning to issue a new edition of the book of Ezekiel, asked you to illustrate this volume, which of Ezekiel's images or symbols would you draw? Explain your drawing.
4. If you were invited by your congregation to preach a sermon on Yom Kippur and you decided to take your text from Ezekiel, which text, quoted in this chapter, would you use? What would you say in Ezekiel's name? Explain what this meant to Ezekiel and his people, and what it means to us today.

[8] 36.26–28

10. PROPHETS AND POETS

Comfort ye, comfort ye my people, saith the Lord . . .

For the mountains may depart
And the hills be removed;
But my kindness shall not depart from thee,
Neither shall My covenant of peace be removed,
Saith the Lord that hath compassion on thee.   (Is. 40.1)

EZEKIEL was not the only prophet in Babylon who sought to comfort and guide the people. There were others. Unfortunately we do not know their names, nor any of the facts of their lives. The best we can do is to try to visualize them through their speeches and poems.

The last twenty-seven chapters of the book of Isaiah — 40 through 66 — are considered by scholars the work of prophets and poets who lived in Babylon with the refugees and who sought to bolster their faith and courage. Bible scholars are in the habit of speaking of "Deutero-Isaiah," that is, "Second Isaiah." Some scholars believe that there may have been a third and perhaps a fourth person whose writings became attached to the writings of Isaiah. We therefore have no stories to tell and no personalities to recall in this chapter of our book. We do, however, have a magnificent collection of poems to read and appreciate.

Three themes dominate this collection of poetry and prophecy.

1. Comfort to a stricken nation;
2. The awesome grandeur of God;
3. Israel is the Servant of the Lord.

We sample this haunting poetry under these three headings, and recall a little history that made these poet-prophets speak as they did.

1. *"Comfort, Comfort Ye My People"*

The time for scolding and warning of God's wrath was past. That had, tragically, come about; the worst that the prophets from Amos through Jeremiah had feared and proclaimed had come true. Now was a time for comforting, healing, emphasizing God's compassion upon His stricken people. God has forgiven; Israel will be delivered. In the mind of the prophet this deliverance has already taken place.

> Comfort ye, comfort ye my people,
> Saith your God.
> Speak ye to the heart of Jerusalem,
> And cry unto her,
> That her time of service is accomplished,
> That her guilt is paid off;
> That she hath received at the Lord's hand
> Double for all her sins.[1]

The poet-prophet hears a voice calling upon unseen powers to prepare the way of the Lord:

> Hark! one calleth:
> "Clear ye in the wilderness the way of the Lord,
> Make straight in the desert
> A highway for our God.

[1] 40.1–2. This chapter is read in synagogues as the *haftarah* on the Sabbath after Tishe b'Ab, the ninth day of the month of Ab. Why?

Every valley shall be lifted up,
And every mountain and hill shall be made low;
And the rugged shall be made level,
And the rough places a plain;
And the glory of the Lord shall be revealed,
And all the flesh shall see it together;
For the mouth of the Lord hath spoken it."

Hark! one saith, "Proclaim!"
And I said, "What shall I proclaim?"
"All flesh is grass,
And the goodliness thereof is as the flower of the field;
The grass withereth, the flower fadeth;
Because the breath of the Lord bloweth upon it.
Surely the people is grass.
The grass withereth, the flower fadeth;
But the word of our God shall stand forever." [2]

A just and merciful God presides over men and nations; He guides and guards Israel. Israel must believe and take heart.

Why sayest thou, O Jacob,
And speakest, O Israel:
"My way is hid from the Lord,
And my right is passed over from my God"?
Hast thou not known? hast thou not heard
That the everlasting God, the Lord,
The Creator of the ends of the earth,
Fainteth not, neither is weary?
His discernment is past searching out.
He giveth power to the faint;
And to him that hath no might He increaseth strength.

Even the youths shall faint and be weary,
And the young men shall utterly fall;

[2] 40.6–8

But they that wait for the Lord shall renew their strength;
They shall mount up with wings as eagles;
They shall run, and not be weary;
They shall walk, and not faint.[3]

Cyrus, the New Liberator

The prophet-poet had good reason for believing as he did that Israel would be restored. First, he was profoundly convinced that a just God governed the world; second, he saw new developments.

A new personality came upon the scene. His name was Cyrus of Persia. He was the new world conqueror. His armies, coming down from the northeast, Media-Persia,* was terrorizing and conquering the world. He was doing what Nebuchadnezzar of Babylon had done before him, and what the Assyrian Sennacherib and Sargon had done before the Babylonians, in the days of Isaiah. In his world-sweeping conquests Cyrus was approaching Babylon. Now it was Babylon's turn to go down before an invader. Cyrus would set the Judean refugees free and permit them to return to their beloved Jerusalem and Judah. The second Isaiah was convinced of that and he sang a song of triumph. This came true. In the year 538 B.C.E. the return of the exiles to Jerusalem began; more followed in the year 520 B.C.E.

The Second Isaiah speaks of Cyrus with rapture. He calls him God's servant.

But now thus saith the Lord that created thee, O Jacob,
And He that formed thee, O Israel:
Fear not, for I have redeemed thee,

---

[3] 40.27–31
* Today part of Iran and Iraq, south west of the Caspian Sea. See map.

I have called thee by thy name, thou art Mine.
When thou passest through the waters, I will be with thee,
And through the rivers, they shall not overflow thee;
When thou walkest through the fire, thou shalt not be burned,
Neither shall the flame kindle upon thee.
For I am the Lord thy God,
The Holy One of Israel, thy Saviour.[4]

God has forgiven, let heaven and earth sing for joy:

> I have blotted out as a thick cloud, thy transgressions,
> And, as a cloud, thy sins;
> Return unto Me, for I have redeemed thee.[5]

Over and over again the prophet-poet returns to his theme
that God has forgiven and deliverance is on the wing; he sees
the messenger of this deliverance coming down from the
mountains, and he sings one of his most glorious songs:

> How beautiful upon the mountains
> Are the feet of the messenger of good tidings,
> That announceth peace, the harbinger of good tidings,
> That announceth salvation;
> That saith unto Zion:
> "Thy God reigneth!"
> Hark, thy watchmen! they lift up the voice,
> Together do they sing;
> For they shall see, eye to eye,
> The Lord returning to Zion.
> Break forth into joy, sing together,
> Ye waste places of Jerusalem;
> For the Lord hath comforted His people,
> He hath redeemed Jerusalem.[6]

[4] 43.1–3
[5] 44.22
[6] 52.7–9

2. *The Awesome Grandeur of God*

The second theme that dominates the prophet's songs is the awesome grandeur of God, Creator of heaven and earth, He Who called the generations into being, and Who governs the lives of men and nations.

> Who hath measured the waters in the hollow of his hand,
> And meted out heaven with a span
> And comprehended the dust of the earth in a measure,
> And weighed the mountains in scales,
> And the hills in a balance?
>
> .   .   .   .
>
> Know ye not?   Hear ye not?
> Hath it not been told you from the beginning?
> Have ye not understood the foundations of the earth?
> It is He that sitteth upon the circle of the earth,
> And the inhabitants thereof are as grasshoppers. . . .
> Lift up your eyes on high
> And see: Who hath created these? [7]

The Judeans must never forget the lovingkindness of God and must never lose heart:

> Fear not, for I have redeemed thee,
> I have called thee by thy name, thou are Mine.
> When thou passest through the waters,
> I will be with thee,
> And through the rivers, they shall not overflow thee.
> For I am the Lord thy God,
> The Holy One of Israel, thy Saviour. [8]

In tragic times — when Crusaders were murdering thousands of Jews, in the days of the Inquisition, in times of

[7] 40.12–26
[8] 43.1–3

Polish-Russian pogroms and Nazi concentration camps — the Jewish people read these words of the prophet-poet of long ago and were comforted.

3. *Israel the Servant of the Lord*

The third theme to which the prophet returns over and over again is Israel as the servant of the Lord, the Chosen People of God, drafted by God himself as His task force, to bring justice, truth and love into the world. Israel is a people dedicated to the Holy One, and is usually referred to as "the Chosen People."

How may Israel serve as God's servant? The question is answered in a famous passage:

> Behold My servant, whom I uphold;
> Mine elect, in whom My soul delighteth;
> I have put My spirit upon him,
> He shall make the right to go forth to the nations.
> He shall not cry, nor lift up,
> Nor cause his voice to be heard in the street.
> A bruised reed shall he not break,
> And the dimly burning wick shall he not quench;
> He shall make the right to go forth according to the truth.
> He shall not fail nor be crushed,
> Till he have set the right in the earth;
> And the isles shall wait for his teaching.[9]

This is not a popular task. It means fighting ignorance, intolerance, hate, poverty, selfishness. That brings sorrow upon the servant of God, even as it brought sorrow upon the prophets; but, again like the prophets, Israel must be faithful

[9] 42.1–4

and courageous, worthy of its prophetic heritage, never yielding to mobs or to tyrants.

> I gave my back to the smiters,
> And my cheek to them that plucked off the hair;
> I hid not my face from shame and spitting.
> For the Lord God will help me;
> Therefore I have not been confounded.[10]

As "Servants of the Lord" Israel must be a just people, just in all its dealings with man and God. Deutero-Isaiah was as intolerant of rituals and ceremonies replacing true religion as were all the other prophets. One of his passages is read in synagogues as the *haftarah* for the Day of Atonement:

Cry aloud, spare not,
Lift up thy voice like a horn,
And declare unto My people their transgression,
And to the house of Jacob their sins.
Yet they seek Me daily,
And delight to know My ways;
As a nation that did righteousness,
And forsook not the ordinance of their God,
They ask of Me righteous ordinances,
They delight to draw near unto God.

'Wherefore have we fasted, and Thou seest not?
Wherefore have we afflicted our soul, and Thou takes no knowl-
    edge?'
Behold, in the day of your fast ye pursue your business,
And exact all your labours.
Behold, ye fast for strife and contention,
And to smite with the fist of wickedness;
Ye fast not this day

[10] 50.4–9

So as to make your voice to be heard on high.
Is such the fast that I have chosen?
The day for a man to afflict his soul?
Is it to bow down his head as a bulrush,
And to spread sackcloth and ashes under him?
Wilt thou call this a fast,
And an acceptable day to the Lord?
Is not *this* the fast that I have chosen?
To loose the fetters of wickedness,
To undo the bands of the yoke,
And to let the oppressed go free,
And that ye break every yoke?
Is it not to deal thy bread to the hungry,
And that thou bring the poor that are cast out to thy house?
When thou seest the naked, that thou cover him,
And that thou hide not thyself from thine own flesh?
Then shall thy light break forth as the morning,
And thy healing shall spring forth speedily;
And thy righteousness shall go before thee,
The glory of the Lord shall be thy rearward.[11]

The spirit of the Lord God is upon me;
Because the Lord hath anointed me
To bring good tidings unto the humble;
He hath sent me to bind up the broken-hearted,
To proclaim liberty to the captives,
And the opening of the eyes to them that are bound;
To proclaim the year of the Lord's good pleasure,
And the day of vengeance * of our God;
To comfort all that mourn;
To appoint unto them that mourn in Zion,
To give unto them a garland for ashes,
The oil of joy for mourning,

[11] 58.1–8
* The rabbis emphasize that *vengeance*, as in this passage, belongs to God, not to any human. Only God has the right to exercise it.

The mantle of praise for the spirit of heaviness;
That they might be called terebinths of righteousness,
The planting of the Lord, wherein He might glory.[12]
And they shall build the old wastes,
They shall raise up the former desolations,
And they shall renew the waste cities,
The desolations of many generations.[13]

The servant of the Lord will rebuild the ruins of the world
and lay the foundations for a better, more just, more loving
world. "It shall come to pass at the end of days."

TOPICS FOR FURTHER STUDY AND DISCUSSION

1. What is meant by "Deutero-Isaiah"?
   Where are these writings to be found?
2. Why is Isaiah 40 read in synagogues on the Sabbath after
   Tishe b'Ab, the ninth day of the month of Ab?
3. What encouraged the prophet to believe that Judah would be
   restored?
4. Add to your "Who's Who" the personalities reported in this
   chapter. Describe them in a sentence or two.
5. Add to your map the names of the countries reported in this
   chapter.
6. To your Chronology add the events reported in this chapter.
7. Find recordings of any of the passages quoted in this chapter
   and play them in class. A good number of these passages
   have been set to music and used as anthems in churches and
   temples. Inquire at a good music shop, or ask a choir director.
8. Compare the poem "who hath measured the waters in the hol-
   low of his hand" with Samuel Taylor Coleridge's "Hymn Before Sun-Rise in the Vale of Chamounix."

[12] 61.1–3
[13] 61.4

9. What did the "Chosen People" mean to Deutero-Isaiah? What can it mean to us today?

10. Compare the Isaiah 61 quotation with the Beatitudes, the first verses of the Sermon on the Mount in the New Testament (Matthew 5.1–12). On which points does Jesus repeat Isaiah?

11. MORE PROPHETS

IN THE first chapter of our book we recalled three prophets who, though they left no books associated with their names, deserve, nevertheless, to be included with the true prophets: Elijah, heavily draped in legend, Nathan and Micaiah ben Imlah. We have studied seven literary prophets: Amos, Hosea, Isaiah, Micah, Jeremiah, Ezekiel, and Deutero-Isaiah (if we may speak of the collection of prophecies and poems in chapters 40–66 in the book of Isaiah as the work of one man). These are the towering figures in Hebrew prophecy — figures that have drawn the admiration of all intelligent men, in all religions, throughout the centuries. Someone has compared them to lightning rods; they brought the fire of God down to earth.

But there were more prophets who are represented in the Bible as the authors of books. Some of these books are only fragments. Eight such additional prophets are in the Bible. We recall them briefly, and cite several passages from their books that have become famous in Jewish tradition. All of them were Judeans; Israel had disappeared in 721 B.C.E., carried off by the Assyrians.

Zephaniah

Zephaniah was the great-great-grandson of King Hezekiah, the King at the time of Isaiah, when Judah was invaded by the Assyrians. He was the only prophet to come from a royal family. Nevertheless, he was sharply critical of the upper classes, as were all the other prophets. He lived at the time of Jeremiah; we do not know if the two men ever associated. He may have had a hand in the Reformation of Josiah in 621 B.C.E. His book consists of three chapters. Reading these we are reminded of Amos: angry attacks on the rich exploiting the poor, the corrupt judges, the ignorant priests, the false prophets, the idolatries of the masses. Like Amos he saw only destruction ahead. Like Isaiah he believed that "a faithful remnant" will save Judah.

> The remnant of Israel shall not do iniquity,
> Nor speak lies,
> Neither shall a deceitful tongue be found in their mouth.[1]

Nahum

Nahum lived about the same time. We know nothing at all of his life. Scholars believe, or infer from his little book, that he spoke his prophecies shortly before Nineveh, the capital of Assyria, fell to the Babylonians in 612 B.C.E. He spoke in furious terms of the Assyrian plunderers. His description of the collapse of the Assyrian armies, which he was sure would take place, is one of the most brilliant bits of writing in the Bible.[2]

Habakkuk

Habakkuk lived at the time of Jeremiah. Again, we do not know if the two men knew each other. He spoke his prophecies between the years 608–597 B.C.E. Like Jeremiah, he was alarmed by the rise of Babylon; like Jeremiah, too, he was

[1] 3.13
[2] 3.19

deeply distressed why God permits such cruelties and injustices to happen. He brooded long over this problem, and, again like Jeremiah, he found the answer — or at least, his comfort — in faith in God. In the long run of history, justice will be done. His most famous sentence is:

The righteous liveth by his faith.[3]

Some answers to moral problems we do not know. Why God permits wars and brutalities, the crushing of innocent people by barbarians, we do not know; but vision we must have at all times, and faith we must not lose or we perish altogether. In one of the choice poems in the Bible, Habakkuk gives us the answer he finally achieved for himself:

> For though the fig-tree shall not blossom,
> Neither shall fruit be in the vines;
> The labour of the olive shall fail,
> And the fields shall yield no food;
> The flock shall be cut off from the fold,
> And there shall be no herd in the stalls;
> Yet I will rejoice in the Lord,
> I will exult in the God of my salvation.[4]

Decree of Cyrus

In the year 539 B.C.E. Cyrus of Media-Persia conquered Babylon, and within a year released the Hebrew refugees. They were permitted to go back to Jerusalem, if they wished. Many refused to migrate back to their homeland; they had prospered and adjusted themselves to their new environment,

[3] Hab. 2.4
[4] 3.17–18

and preferred to remain, but they did send money and assistance to those who did return. Their conduct reminds us of the conduct of American Jews who prefer to remain in America, where they are integrated in the life of the country, but do give financial help to those who seek to build the State of Israel. In the year 538 B.C.E. a group of refugees returned to Jerusalem, under the leadership of Zerubbabel. This history is reported in the books of Ezra and Nehemiah. These men led in the rebuilding of Jerusalem, the restoration of the Temple, and the rehabilitation of the people. In the year 444 B.C.E. Ezra called a national convention and read to the assembled people the first edition of the Torah, to which they pledged their loyalty anew.

Haggai and Zechariah

Two prophets sought to rouse the people to the rebuilding of the Temple, Haggai and Zechariah. Haggai's booklet is only two chapters. Zechariah's is much longer, fourteen chapters. Both men spoke in the year 520 B.C.E. Their books do not measure up to the lofty greatness of the major prophets. They were too concerned with the rebuilding of the priestly Temple and its sacrifices, which the great prophets did not like at all. But from Zechariah comes a sentence which is one of the loftiest pronouncements in the Bible and Judaism:

Not by might and not by power but by My spirit, saith the Lord.[5]

Men and nations do not live by brute force; men and nations find their security in organizing their affairs and living their lives in the moral law, which is the spirit of God.

[5] Zech. 4.6

In the year 516 B.C.E. the Temple was sufficiently rebuilt to be rededicated. They who had wept by the waters of Babylon now sang a psalm of thanksgiving:

> When the Lord brought back those that returned to Zion,
> We were like unto them that dream.
> Then was our mouth filled with laughter,
> And our tongue with singing;
> Then said they among the nations:
> "The Lord hath done great things with these."
> The Lord hath done great things with us;
> We are rejoiced.[6]

Obadiah — Joel — Malachi

Three prophets may belong to this period.

Of Obadiah, whose "book" is only one small chapter, we know nothing at all. The little fragment is a violent attack on Edom. The Edomites were the descendants of Esau, brother of Jacob. Nevertheless, though Judah and Edom were brother nations, there was bitter hatred between them.

Joel may or may not belong to this time. Scholars are in wide disagreement as to his dates. His book consists of only three small chapters. They describe vividly the calamities that had befallen Judah — drought, famine, the harvests burned into dust, the beasts perishing, the pitiless heat setting the forests on fire, locusts swarming over the land. Joel saw in that God's punishment. But God is just; He will have compassion. The rains will return, the earth will revive.

> The Lord will be a refuge to His people,
> And a stronghold to the children of Israel.[7]

[6] Ps. 126.1–3
[7] 4.16

The prophet whose booklet completes the books of the Hebrew prophets is a man who is known to us by the name of Malachi. That may not have been his real name. The word Malachi, in Hebrew, means "my messenger." The word occurs in the opening sentence of the first chapter of Malachi, and the word came to designate the prophet's name. Like Ezekiel, he sought to revive enthusiasm among the discouraged people.

One of the most frequently quoted passages is Malachi's plea for the brotherhood of all men and races:

Have we not all one Father?
Hath not one God created us?
Why do we deal treacherously every man against his brother,
Profaning the covenant of our fathers? [8]

To the suffering and despairing people, to the men and women who had lost courage because of the many troubles that had come upon them, he spoke of God's mercy and lovingkindness, even as Hosea had spoken:

But unto you that fear My name,
Shall the sun of righteousness arise with healing on its wings.[9]

Jonah — Ruth

Malachi completes our list of prophets; but there were more prophets than are represented by the prophetic books in the Bible.

The book of Jonah is a parable. It must not be read as history, nor as biography. It is a story, written by a man un-

[8] 2.10
[9] 3.20

known to us, but who must be listed among our great prophets. By means of this short novel, the prophet-author seeks to teach a triple lesson: *First*, God is the Lord of all peoples, Hebrews or Assyrians, Israelites or Edomites. God commands a Hebrew prophet to carry His message to the heathen Assyrians, the very people who had robbed and plundered Israel. Why? Because God is a God of justice and of mercy and He knows no national, no racial favorites. *Second*, God is everywhere; there is no place in creation where He is not. Poor, stupid little Jonah, trying to run away from the presence of the Almighty! In Joppa or in Tarshish, on the sea or at the bottom of the ocean, He is there! And He speaks and commands words of justice, and compassion, urging men to repent of their evil ways and merit His forgiveness. *Third*, he urges the lesson of repentance. If the people repent, God will forgive them and save them. The rabbis decreed that the book of Jonah be read in synagogues on the Day of Atonement, since it teaches such a powerful lesson in repentance. A great scholar has written that the little book of Jonah is "the triumph of Judaism."

The book of Ruth, like the book of Jonah, is a parable. Again an unknown writer, whom we would delight to place among the prophets if we knew his name, protested against what we today call racial hatreds. He wrote his book at the time of Ezra-Nehemiah, when the refugees who had returned from Babylon were trying to rebuild Jerusalem and the Temple.

While the Judeans were in Babylon, their country back home was overrun by squatters; they were people of various tribes and races. In re-establishing the state and the Temple Ezra could not tell who was a Judean and who not. They

had inter-married so thoroughly. One of the reforms Ezra
and his associates tried to enforce was for Hebrew men
to divorce their non-Hebrew wives, thus re-establishing the
purity of the Hebrew stock. We have no records to show
that this was ever enforced. Someone wrote a short novel
protesting against this. Men loved their wives then as now,
race or no race.

The author gives us a charming picture of a devoted, fine
woman by the name of Ruth. She was a Moabite. Bitter race
hatred existed between the Moabites and the Judeans. The
author presents this Moabite young woman as an exemplary
person — loyal, devoted, fine in every way. That was his way
of fighting race prejudice in his time. From this Moabite in
time came King David, he writes romantically, and from King
David's family some day, in God's own good time, say the
rabbis of the Talmud, will come the Messiah, who will free
the world of its hatred, evils, and violence and establish the
Kingdom of God on earth. In Christian tradition too, Ruth
is a person of sanctity. Jesus, it is reported, was of the stock of
Jesse, father of David; hence it is from Ruth that Jesus came.
The rabbis of the Talmud even decreed that the book of Ruth
be read in synagogues on the festival of Shavuoth. This festival celebrates the giving of the Law to Moses on Mount Sinai.
The people accepted this Torah and thereby became God's
people. The non-Jewish Ruth too accepted God's commandments as loyally as did the Israelites at Mount Sinai: hence
Ruth is as much an Israelitish woman as were they whose ancestors had stood at Sinai.

The man who wrote this charming story was a prophet and
fully deserves an honored place among the prophets.

There were still more prophets, though we do not know

them by name and have no writings associated with their names. Thus, for example, the man or men who wrote the story of Abraham and the sacrifice of Isaac, or of Abraham trying to save Sodom and Gemorrah,[10] were prophets: they were concerned with the justice and love of God in the lives of men and communities. The spirit of the prophets is in much of the laws of Moses, especially in the book of Deuteronomy, and even in the book of Leviticus. "Thou shalt love thy neighbor as thyself," [11] or "Let freedom ring throughout the land unto all the inhabitants thereof," [12] or "The stranger (or *foreigner*) that sojourneth with you shall be unto you as the home-born among you, and thou shalt love him as thyself; for ye were strangers in the land of Egypt," [13] are out of the heart of Hebrew prophecy.

TOPICS FOR FURTHER STUDY AND DISCUSSION

1. Explain the sentence: "Someone has compared them (the prophets) *to lightning rods;* they brought the fire of God down to earth."
2. Add the personalities presented in this chapter to your "Who's Who" in their chronologic order.
3. Add the historic events referred to in this chapter to your Chronology.
4. Explain the following:
   a) "a remnant of Israel"
   b) "The righteous liveth by his faith."
   c) "Not by might, not by power, but by My spirit, saith the Lord."

[10] Gen. 22.18
[11] Lev. 19.18
[12] Lev. 25.10
[13] Lev. 19.34

    d) "Have we not all One Father?

       Hath not one God created us?"

5. Tell the story of Ruth in the form of acts, or scenes, in the manner of a drama.

    Why is the book of Ruth read in synagogues on Shavuoth?

6. Tell the story of Jonah in the form of acts, or scenes, in the manner of a drama.

    Why is the book of Jonah read in synagogues on the Day of Atonement?

12. IT SHALL COME TO PASS

REFLECTING on all the prophets we have studied, we observe that each one of them spoke in his own manner. Nevertheless, they had certain features in common. All of them were dominated by one and the same passion: to speak the will of God in the affairs of men and nations. That is what the word "prophet" means; one who is the spokesman for another, and the "other" for whom the Hebrew prophets spoke was God. That was the driving passion of their lives. Nothing else mattered. Whether they were popular or not, hated or not, meant nothing to them. One thing mattered and one thing only: the will of God. And they spoke their minds without fear, and without compromise.

"Thus saith the Lord," is the refrain in all their speaking. They were the spokesmen of the Eternal, and they were in deadly earnest.

We notice, also, that the prophets spoke in times of great peril, when their nation was facing a crisis. They addressed themselves to the specific evils of their time that needed correction. They did not speak in general terms. Isaiah, for example, spoke when the Assyrian invaders were loose in the world and invaded Judah, when his own King was making foolish and dangerous alliances; Jeremiah spoke when the Scythians were about to attack Jerusalem, or, more especially, when the Babylonian armies were marching against Judah, and finally invaded it. To Jeremiah it meant the crack of doom over the country he loved. Ezekiel spoke to people who were deeply grieved, confused and frightened. The prophets, that is, spoke in practical terms, in the light of specific events, in troubled times.

We notice, further, that all the prophets peered into the future and foretold certain developments; but, we must not fail to notice, they were not fortune tellers. We noted in our opening chapter that they foretold the future the way a meteorologist foretells the weather for the day, or for several days, or a week ahead: they observed causes and were sure that certain consequences would follow inevitably. If the leaders of a country are stupid or corrupt, if the judges take bribes, if the priests are ignorant and exploit the ignorance of the people, if the poor, the sick, are neglected, revolution and chaos follow. And, like the weatherman who sees a hurricane in the making hopes that his prediction may prove false, the prophets too hoped that their prognostications of evil times would prove false. The point is that they were not concerned with their expertness in foretelling, but were trying — desperately — to change the conditions and circumstance so that the evil they saw on the horizon would not come about.

A favorite expression of the prophet Isaiah is, "It shall come to pass at the end of days." Beyond the evils of the times he saw a juster, better world in the future. A faithful remnant there will be, and these just and compassionate men will bring about a better world. Thus he dreamed of a time when nations would beat their swords into plowshares and learn war no more, when "they shall not hurt nor destroy in all my holy mountain for the earth shall be filled with the knowledge of God as the waters cover the sea." [1]

Their dreams were long, long dreams; their visions were on

[1] 11.9

the horizon of the generations yet unborn. They dreamed of the kingdom of God on earth.

Some of their predictions came true. Unfortunately, the predictions of terror and calamity, invasion and dispersion of Judah, did come true. Isaiah, as we have noted, lived through four invasions of his beloved country; Jeremiah lived through the agonies of his nation conquered and carried off into exile. But their predictions of a more just world on a fairer earth, under more peaceful heavens, is also coming true. Men of vision and high ideals among all peoples — Jews and Christians and Mohammedans and people of other religions, of white and black and brown races — are laboring for a peaceful world when, in the words of Isaiah, "nations shall beat their swords into plowshares and learn war no more."

In the State of Israel today — reestablished more than two thousand years after the prophets spoke — on a hill known as Ramat-Rahel stands a statue of Mother Rachel, beloved wife of Jacob, mother of Joseph and Benjamin. To the left as one faces the statue one sees the hilly wilderness of Judah, where David pastured his sheep and composed his psalms; beyond, on the far horizon, one sees Mount Nebo, from which Moses looked longingly on the Promised Land, and where he lies buried.

The statue is that of a woman holding one child to her breast and another by the hand. On the pedestal is an inscription taken from the prophet Jeremiah:

Thus saith the Lord;
Refrain thy voice from weeping,
And thine eyes from tears;
For thy work shall be rewarded, saith the Lord;
And they shall come back from the land of the enemy.

> And there is hope for thy future, saith the Lord;
> And thy children shall return to their own border.[2]

One finds himself fascinated that words spoken by the prophet back in the year 586 B.C.E., or shortly before, could come true some twenty-five hundred years later. And one recalls other prophecies, such as Isaiah's:

> I will bring thy seed from the east,
> And gather thee from the west;
> I will say to the north: "Give up,"
> And to the south: "Keep not back,
> Bring my sons from afar,
> And my daughters from the ends of the earth." [3]
>
> .   .   .   .
>
> And the ransomed of the Lord shall return,
> And come with singing unto Zion,
> And everlasting joy shall be on their heads;
> They shall obtain gladness and joy,
> And sorrow and sighing shall flee away.[4]

But the prophets dreamed of more than external events when they spoke "It shall come to pass at the end of days." Isaiah's vision of nations beating their swords into plowshares has not yet come true; but, our prayers and our labors dictate it. "It *shall* come to pass at the end of days." Jeremiah's prophecy that the security of a people rests not on arms and weapons and buildings but on right conduct between every man and his neighbor is still to be realized. His dream that a covenant with God will be engraved on the hearts and minds

[2] 31.16–17
[3] 43.6
[4] 51.11

of men is still to be achieved. For that we labor and pray and hope. "It shall come to pass at the end of days."

TOPICS FOR FURTHER STUDY AND DISCUSSION

1. Combine your "Who's Who" with the Chronology and add, in a parallel column, brackets representing the prophets we have studied in their proper historic positions.
2. Explain four characteristics of all the prophets, and cite examples from their books.
3. Make a list of the memory passages you have committed to memory. Can you recite them?